Set Yourself Free:
Reon Schutte's 10 Principles
to Break Out of Your Personal Prison
through The Power of Choice

Set Yourself Free:
Reon Schutte's 10 Principles
to Break Out of Your Personal Prison
through The Power of Choice

Reon Schutte
with
Maggie Kuhn Jacobus

NEW YORK

Set Yourself Free:
Reon Schutte's 10 Principles to Break Out of Your Personal Prison through The Power of Choice

For security reasons, most names in Reon's story have either been changed or individuals were not named. Permission was received from Phillip-Niel Albertyn to use his name. Originally published by HenschelHAUS Publishing, Inc. under ISBN: 978159598-152-3

ISBN 978-1-61448-380-9 paperback
ISBN 978-1-61448-381-6 eBook
Library of Congress Control Number: 2012950939

Morgan James Publishing
The Entrepreneurial Publisher
5 Penn Plaza, 23rd Floor
New York City, New York 10001
(212) 655-5470 office • (516) 908-4496 fax
www.MorganJamesPublishing.com

Cover Design by:
Rachel Lopez
www.r2cdesign.com

Interior Design by:
Bonnie Bushman
bonnie@caboodlegraphics.com

In an effort to support local communities, raise awareness and funds, Morgan James Publishing donates a percentage of all book sales for the life of each book to Habitat for Humanity Peninsula and Greater Williamsburg.

Get involved today, visit
www.MorganJamesBuilds.com.

*For all those living in personal prisons who desire
to break free and live engaged, vibrant lives.*

ACKNOWLEDGMENTS

REON'S ACKNOWLEDGMENTS

There are so many people to thank. The story I share here is just a small part of a larger one that involves hundreds of people. I am grateful to Phillip Albertyn and my entire support group, to those in the various governments and organizations around the world who worked on my behalf, and to my fellow prisoners and the guards at Chikurubi.

Thank you to all the individuals and organizations who helped me once I was released, and to those individuals and organizations who started me on and have supported me in my speaking career, including Young Presidents Organization, Entrepreneur's Organization, Derek Watts, TV Azteca, Matt Stewart, Tom and Shauna Mabey, Dale Williams, Bahman Shafa, and countless, countless others.

Thank you to Maggie Kuhn Jacobus for helping me put my story in writing and to articulate the lessons I learned.

MAGGIE'S ACKNOWLEDGEMENTS

Thank you to my family and friends for their love and support while on this journey. Thank you to Reon for entrusting me to put his story into written form and to interpret the lessons he learned into practical application to make them accessible to all. I have learned a great deal in the process. Thank you to all those individuals who have supported and encouraged me to write this book.

INTRODUCTION

The teacher who is indeed wise does not bid you to enter the house of his wisdom, but rather leads you to the threshold of your mind.
—**Kahlil Gibran**

This book is the result of requests from you and the 1 million+ people Reon Schutte has spoken to around the world since his release from Zimbabwe's Chikurubi prison in 2004.

"How do I put your message into practice?" has been an oft-asked question. "What was your methodology for transformation?" is another familiar query. "Do I need to give up everything I own in order to be happy?" some ask, half-hopeful, half-terrified to hear the answer.

Most everyone is seeking happiness, fulfillment, and inner peace. This can only be because so many of us feel *un*happy, *un*fulfilled, and anything but peace-filled.

As such, the pursuit of happiness has become a major industry, with hundreds of books and seminars dedicated to telling us how to get it. Problem is, it's not out there to get. It is not a thing, a place, a person. It is not an amount of money, a particular job, a status. We all know of people who have none of those things...but are happy. And we all also know people who have *all* of those things...yet are *un*happy. How is that so?

Reon's story illustrates many universal truths and this is one of them: you can choose to be happy, despite your circumstances. Happiness is a *choice*.

We may *know* this, but how do we put it into practice? Back to your requests for methodology.

Reon never set out to create a methodology for happiness or for personal transformation. He simply *is* personal transformation, and offers his story as an example of what is possible within each of us.

Yet he understands your requests for more detail on the "how" of his transformation and so we've created this book for you. Reon entrusted me to share his story in his voice and then to articulate what he learned in a way that makes his experience relevant to each of us in our daily lives. Based on hundreds of hours of interviews and conversations I've conducted with Reon, workshops we have presented together, and the questions and comments from thousands of people around the world who have heard him speak, I've written this book to illustrate the 10 Principles, or major lessons, he learned through his ordeal and that he continues to practice each day. The Principles are guideposts for each of us to use to break out of our personal prisons and achieve our own freedom. Reon came to these truths in a way far outside the realm of experience for most of us and perhaps that is why his story impacts us so.

As different as his story is from your own daily existence, however, the Principles are universal and are thus ones everyone can use. Reon's story is merely a fascinating one, though, unless you *take action*, unless you put the Principles into practice. Not just once. But every day. Every *minute* of every day. If there's anything I've learned from Reon, it's that there is no quick trick for transformation. The metamorphosis comes about through repeated action.

No one can do transformation for you and no one can really give you anything that you don't already have to work the magic. You are the base metal, the alchemist, and the gold all in one. You simply need to recognize that, accept responsibility for having the power of choice to create your life, choose to engage that inner knowledge...and then take action.

And that's the purpose of this book: to help you dig in and start the work. It's about stoking the fire, so you can undergo your own personal alchemical transmutation from base metal into gold. Think of Reon and his story as tinder for your own fire, not the fire itself.

How to Use this Book

This book is part story, part guidebook, part workbook. The most effective way to use it is to first read *Section One: Imprisonment*, an overview of Reon's personal story, particularly his odyssey as a prisoner of war in one of Zimbabwe's most notoriously brutal prisons. The story sets the context for the Principles.

Section Two: Freedom is kicked off with an introduction, followed by the 10 Principles--the major lessons Reon gleaned through his ordeal and beyond. In this section, we delve further into Reon's journey to mine each major lesson.

Following each Principle is a "workbook" section. Drawing on my experience as a life coach, I have developed guiding questions and exercises for you to use to go deeper into each Principle to determine what it means for you and how you can use it as a tool for transformation. Each Principle and its exercises comprise a chapter.

The 10 Principles do not necessarily need to be read and worked on in order. After reading Section One, you can start right away to exercise your Power of Choice and decide which Principle you want to delve into first and go from there, moving forward and backward through the Principles. Most of the Principles do relate to one another, however, so you may find benefit in going through them in the order in which they are placed in this book, but that is not necessary.

Make this book your own journal and journey to freedom. Carry it with you so you can make notes in it as you become conscious of a choice you've made, or as thoughts come to you that allow you to shift your experience of your circumstances. Reread it, and add new thoughts or ideas to your original ones. Gather a small group together to discuss the lessons and share your interpretation and insights. Observe your own evolution and, as you become more and more aware of the choices before you and the choices you make, notice how your life unfolds.

Not liking the way things are going? Make another choice, re-evaluate your response. Reread Reon's story. Reread the lessons. I've heard Reon tell his story hundreds of times to audiences around the world, and each time, I hear something new or understand something I didn't before. What you take away from his story today I guarantee will evolve into deeper and deeper understanding as you go through this journey and use this guidebook to reach a deep and real state of happiness and peace, the type that comes only from within and that cannot be shaken, despite what happens to you or around you.

— **Maggie Kuhn Jacobus**

PART I:

IMPRISONMENT

AFRICA

1 - THE GAMBIA
2 - GUINEA BISSAU
3 - EQUATORIAL GUINEA
4 - RWANDA
5 - BURUNDI
6 - MALAWI
7 - LESOTHO

REON'S STORY

'm going to tell you a story. It's not something I read or studied or
heard about from someone else. I lived it.

I want to start by telling you a bit about where I come from and
some history of my people.

I'm an Afrikaner. Afrikaners are an ethnic group that evolved in
South Africa, starting in the mid-1600s. Over a period of about 150
years, various Europeans, particularly Dutch, Germans, and French,
settled along the southern tip of the African continent—the Cape of
Good Hope—to provide supplies to the shipping companies passing
on the trade routes. Other ethnicities also settled there, including
Portuguese, Italians, Greeks, Spaniards, Scots, Irishmen, and Poles, to
name a few.

Over several hundred years, as these settlers intermarried, a new
ethnic group emerged with its own culture, customs, and language—
the Afrikaners. Afrikaners are of a different ethnicity than the South
Africans of English descent, whose first language is English. Typical of
all Afrikaner children of my era, *Afrikaans* was my first language. Zulu
and Xhosa (languages of two black tribes) were my second and third,
also learned in childhood. I didn't learn to speak English until I was a

young adult in the military. There, I learned English and a half-dozen other languages as part of my training for undercover work.

Afrikaaner is the Afrikaans word for "African." I am a white African. My people are one of more than a dozen different ethnic groups and five distinct races that call South Africa home. The aboriginal Khoisan are the only group who can claim to be the original inhabitants of Southern Africa. The black Africans migrated south from the northern part of the continent, the whites came from Europe, the majority of Indians and Asians were indentured laborers brought by the British, and the Coloreds evolved in Africa as other races intermingled.

Legend has it that the first person to declare himself an Afrikaner was Hendrik Biebouw, who, in March 1707, is reputed to have stated, *"Ik ben een Afrikander."* ("I am an African.") He echoes the sentiments of all Afrikaners, and probably all the other ethnicities that call South Africa home.

Although my distant ancestors are from Europe, I am not. You could think of an Afrikaner the way citizens born in the United States consider themselves as being American. Unless they are Native American, their ancestors came from somewhere else. Yet the passport they carry, the flag they salute, and the nationality they list on their immigration forms is "American." Despite the common assumption that Afrikaners are simply displaced Dutch ("Dutchman" is a grave insult that the South African English kids liked to hurl at us), I actually could not claim to be Dutch or any other European ethnicity, even if I wanted to.

I know this first hand, because as I lay captive in a Zimbabwean prison, I appealed to various European governments for assistance, as did Amnesty International and other human rights organizations on my behalf. The European countries all essentially said, "You are not one of us. You are an Afrikaner, your people are from Africa, and thus you can't claim citizenship by descent."

We Afrikaners are a fiercely proud, stubborn, hard-working people. We don't give up easily and we don't take kindly to being under other's rules. Over time, my people evolved from providing refreshment along the coasts to passing trade ships, to moving inland, owning land and being farmers, living as far away from the rules and regulations of the original coastal colonies as possible.

Unfortunately for the Afrikaners, diamonds, gold, and other precious resources were discovered on our lands and England essentially said, "Those belong to us." A war ensued, the first Anglo-Boer War. The Afrikaners pioneered some of the first guerilla war tactics in this conflict and it's one of the reasons my people won, even though there were considerably fewer of them than British. The British came back with more people, more and bigger guns, and employed brutal tactics like the "scorched earth" policy of destroying civilian homes, land and crops, leaving the innocents caught in the middle of war to suffer the greatest.

The British also pioneered a different warfare tactic: concentration camps. An estimated 120,000 Afrikaners, mostly women and children, were put into such camps, and as many as 30,000 of them died there. That was one of the earliest uses of concentration camps in modern warfare.

In 1902, the British won the second Anglo-Boer War. The Cape and Natal colonies, as well as the republics of Orange Free State and Transvaal, were lumped together into a British Empire dominion known as the Union of South Africa.

Afrikaners don't give up...and we don't easily forget, either. Even today in South Africa, you'll find Afrikaners who don't—or won't—speak English despite, or perhaps because of, being an English colony for decades and before that, subjected to the atrocities inflicted by that nation on our ancestors.

In 1961, South Africa gained its independence from Britain and became the Republic of South Africa. The political power stayed with the white minority, the Afrikaners, who had earlier made an uneasy peace with their English foes. As with most African nations upon receiving independence from whatever European nation had ruled them for decades or centuries prior, the door for political instability was opened when England's Queen Elizabeth II ceased to be South Africa's head of state. A power struggle that had been brewing for decades gained ground, and a civil war soon broke out.

That year, 1961, also happens to be the year in which I was born. So I was born into war and grew up in a country at war. The first time I experienced a peaceful country was at the age of 43.

———

We don't choose who we are born as, what nationality, what country, what culture, what religion. That is God-given. I happened to be born a white Afrikaner to a very poor family in a country embarking on a violent 30-year conflict that eventually involved and overlapped with conflicts in more than a dozen other African nations, including Angola, Mozambique, Zimbabwe, and South West Africa (now Namibia).

I was born on the 26th of February in a small town called Brakpan. It was a typical rural, conservative, South African Afrikaner town of the 1960s. We had no TV then; in fact, we didn't get TV in South Africa until the 1970s, and then it was black and white, with government-approved programming just a few hours every day.

The original European settlers in South Africa had mostly been Dutch Calvinists and, hundreds of years later, their strict, conservative, puritanical mindset still dominated every aspect of our culture. When

I was growing up, I never saw a photo of a woman in a bikini; that was considered pornographic. Imagine my shock when I returned to my country in 2004, after 18 years of fighting a guerilla war mostly in the jungles and twelve years, eight months in prison, and saw "pornography" plastered all over public billboards.

I was one of four children, the second youngest. We were three brothers and one sister. For the first five or six years of my life, I lived with my grandmother, my mother's mother. The rest of the family traveled around with my father, who did construction work, among other odd jobs.

I don't recall ever being given an explanation as to why I lived with Granny while my siblings were all with my parents. I can only surmise that because of our extreme poverty, my parents desperately needed one less mouth to feed. Since I was old enough to walk and work, but not so old as to be difficult, I was the one who went to Granny. At the time I fancied it was because I was her favorite. Perhaps I was.

One can never really remember the first years of one's life, but the memory flashes I have of mine are mostly good ones.

Granny and I lived on her pension in a little house across the street from the railway line. The house used to rattle several times a day and throughout the night when the trains rolled by. I loved the haunting sound of the train whistle and the clatter of the train on the tracks. It soothed me to sleep every night.

At dawn, Granny would wake me to gather food for the day. Before heading out, I would stumble half-asleep into the chilly kitchen to start a fire in the wood stove. I would also light a few candles for light to dress by, since it was still pitch black outside and we had no electricity. Then I would grab my sling shot and Granny and I would walk out, hand in hand, in search of food in the growing light of dawn. She'd forage for wild spinach; I'd shoot birds with my sling shot.

Whatever food we found, Granny would then spend hours transforming it into a delicious meal. To this day, I'm constantly in search of the perfect, proper Afrikaner stew or soup or sausage. No one cooks like an Afrikaner.

With Granny cooking, I'd grab my wagon and walk as fast as I could to the dump. I was in a hurry to get there so I could return as quickly as possible to eat. At the dump, I continued foraging, this time for copper wire and metal scraps that Granny could turn in for money.

From time to time, the rest of the family would come to visit. I remember them arriving in a big, old Valiant four-door car. Sometimes there would be lots of presents, other times they would come and stay with us for a while and we would all live on Granny's pension, while my old man looked for another job. He was a guy who always had a job, but could never keep it for long.

At age six, as is tradition in my culture, I was given my first hunting rifle by my father and taught to clean and dress wild game in the field. Also as is tradition, I was given a test of my ability—I was sent out into the bush with my rifle and three bullets and told not to come back until I had three kill. Three bullets, three kill. Anything less was a waste of precious bullets...and failure. I succeeded. Afrikaners are some of the best snipers in the world and perhaps now you know why. By age 14, I could shoot a bull's eye up to half a mile away, about the maximum distance a .303 could fire.

Also when I was around age six, Granny sold her house and she and I started traveling with the family. My memories of this next phase of childhood are of constantly moving from one place to another with the family. I'm told that I was in more than two dozen different schools over a period of about five years. The amazing thing is that I never failed one year.

Numerous times in the middle of the night, my father and mother would pack us four children, my granny, and as many of our possessions that they could fit in the Valiant, and with no explanation, we would be off, Johnny Cash crooning on the radio, my dad singing along in high spirits, as if we were heading off on a vacation. By morning, we'd be in a new town, starting over again. We lived wherever my father managed to find a job.

There were many times we lived on nothing more than *pap*—a stiff cornmeal porridge—and wild spinach. Sometimes we ended up in government-subsidized housing. My old man was a good guy and did the best he could in life. Such a lifestyle might not be the right thing by other people's standards, but it was the best by his. He taught us to work with our hands right from the start, and I remember being seven years old or so and having to work through the nights with my two older brothers, helping my old man with a carpentry project.

Thinking back, it must have been a very hard and stressful life for my mother. I remember her as a good woman, and an amazing one. She never gave up, and managed under the most difficult circumstances to feed, clothe, and teach us moral principles.

When I was ten or so, I ran away from home for the first time. I left for school one morning like usual, barefoot and searching for fresh cowpats to jump into to warm up my feet, which were freezing in the early morning frost. My family was in one of those phases of having little to eat and we were living in a relative's garage. Hopping from cowpat to cowpat that morning, a thought occurred to me: *I could lessen the burden on my family by taking off.* I don't think I really intended to go away forever because I really loved my mom and sister. I remember I had this dream of going away and returning some day when I was all grown up, very rich and successful, and coming to get my mom and sis and giving them everything they wanted.

The idea of leaving home took hold and, instead of going to school that day, I hopped a train and started my first of several walkabouts around Africa. After several months, however, I got picked up by the cops and sent back to my parents. This cycle went on for a couple of years, with me progressively getting into more and more trouble.

At the age of twelve, I ran away for good. I became a street kid and ended up joining one of the biggest gangs in Cape Town. In just a few short years, I had evolved from a sweet boy picking spinach with my granny to being one of the most fearless and feared gang members in the country. Eventually, that reputation caught up with me and I was sent to a juvenile military detention center, where I spent the next four years of my life. It was an abusive, raw existence filled with endless drilling and marching, I suppose to drum the devil out of us.

At that time, it was law that every white, male South African had to give two years of military service to his country immediately upon leaving school. One could refuse conscription and go to prison for five years. Although I now know that some people opted to be conscientious objectors, when I was a teenager, I didn't know anyone who did that and it never crossed my mind to do so, either. No Afrikaner I knew would have refused to serve and protect his country.

Military conscription offered another, very specific opportunity for me—a way out of the cruel life at the detention center.

So, at the age of 16, I entered the South African Defense Force (SADF) to serve my country. Six months later, I was carrying an automatic rifle and was posted at the Caprivi Strip along the Zambezi River. This was the late 1970s and the height of various African wars that became intermingled with our own, including the Rhodesian Bush War, the Angolan Civil War, and the South West Africa-Angolan Border War. The Caprivi Strip was key in those conflicts and was also utilized by the African National Congress (ANC) to mount their attacks against South Africa, so the action was hot. We experienced intense guerilla fighting—sporadic raids and sniper attacks—which kept us on eternal guard and left our teenaged nerves jangled.

While racial inequality and segregation—known in Afrikaans as *apartheid*, "separateness," or probably even more directly translated as "apartness"—were the most publicized aspects of the South African image and conflict to the Western world, the struggle was not so black and white to those of us doing the actual fighting.

To us, the color of one's skin meant far less than the color of one's uniform and the make of one's gun, for the opposition was trained, funded, outfitted, and armed by the Communist bloc countries, primarily the Soviet Union and Cuba. The wars in Africa were fronts of a worldwide war being waged by the Soviets. I met many Cubans, Soviets, and Chinese in the field, in addition to the AK-47-toting black Africans from various tribes and political factions. Although we rarely encountered them in the field, East German (GDR) soldiers also had a significant presence, particularly in Angola. The influence of these outsiders is still felt in South Africa today; decades after the war has ended, you can still hear black males addressing one another as "Comrade," even though most of them never fought in the conflicts.

I also fought in my battalion alongside black Africans, all of us identifying the other as friend primarily by the weapon used. Early on, it was the FN FAL (*fusil automatique léger,* or light automatic rifle), a popular Cold War-era weapon known as "the right arm of the Free World" because of its widespread use among many of NATO's armed forces. Later we used R4s, a South African-made version of the Israeli Galil ARM assault rifle.

The bottom line was, if the other guy had the wrong gun and the wrong uniform, he was the enemy.

The opposition factions set up their terrorist training camps in African countries outside of South Africa, so my job as a 16-year-old solder was patrolling boarders in the politically charged Caprivi Strip, and later in my career, secretly crossing borders.

After six months of basic training and 18 months of service, my conscription duty was finished. I had the option of going back into civil society and finding some kind of job, or becoming a permanent soldier. I liked being a soldier. I was proud to wear my country's uniform. I was proud to defend my country. I liked the discipline and the sense of purpose and honor.

Later in life, I came to realize just how complex the issues were, that there were true raging racists, as well as authentic freedom fighters, involved in the wars. I also came to know that the vast majority of people actually fighting the conflicts were merely pawns of their leaders or even of different countries, or were gangsters masquerading as fighters for a cause, and that the biggest victims were the same as my own ancestors had experienced centuries prior: the innocent civilians, mostly women and children, caught in the middle. But at age 17, I wasn't so wise. At the time, being a soldier was a job, and a prestigious one at that.

I decided to stay in the military and applied to the Special Forces. I made the grade and at age 18, became one of the youngest Special Forces soldiers in SADF history.

For the next 16 years of my life, I fought a guerilla war in 13 African countries. I was a member of the 5th recce and was later recruited for a highly secretive unit known as the Civil Cooperation Bureau (CCB). My specialty was cross-border raids into the enemy terrorist training camps.

In 1990, the power in South Africa was starting to be handed over to the black majority. We were given orders to go into various African countries, close up operations, and come home. After three decades of conflict, the war in South Africa was ending.

I was sent to six countries to close things up, the last one being Zimbabwe, a place I'd been to many times during the war. When I reported the mission accomplished, I was told there was yet one more final mission in Zim. I was anxious to get back home and move into civilian life. Eighteen years of war, the last several undercover, had taken their toll on me physically and emotionally, although I probably wouldn't have put it that way at the time. I had also become disillusioned with my government and its military practices. From my perspective, many of our tactics had become as senseless and brutal as the enemy's. As the war dragged on, it seemed to no longer be about a cause, but about personal vendettas and agendas and greed on both sides.

Nothing made sense to me anymore. I was ready to move away from the relentless and senseless pounding of death, horror, and war and transition into peaceful civilian life. But this last mission was one I couldn't say no to: three of our guys had been captured a few years back and were being held in a Zimbabwean prison. I was to meet two other contacts there and the three of us were to rescue our guys. I took the mission.

The intel was that the three captives were scheduled to be transported in a police wagon from prison to court on a specific day at a specific time. We were to hit the truck en route, rescue them, and get out.

When we hit the truck, we found not our three guys, but about 30 Zim Special Forces waiting for us. We had been sold out. My two buddies were killed; I was wounded and captured.

I was detained for two years at Harare remand prison and then, in 1992, in a military tribunal, I was sentenced to 26 years of imprisonment in Zimbabwe as a South African spy. I was a Special Forces soldier and a member of a secret, government-sanctioned unit for which I did covert missions, but I was not a spy. But this was the end of the Cold War and the public and media were crazy for spies, so the term stuck. Even upon my release more than a decade later, the South African media were still calling me a spy.

In Africa, a 26-year prison sentence is a death sentence. As a rule, prisons there are overcrowded, filthy, violent, death camps. Human rights don't exist. Most inmates don't last more than a few years, if they're lucky. Or *un*lucky, really. Many people would rather die than endure an African prison. I saw guys do just that: come in, 250 pounds and healthy, sit down, and die within a few months. They weren't killed; they gave up, probably to get the misery over with.

I was taken to a prison called Chikurubi, located about 20 kilometers (12 or so miles) outside Zimbabwe's capital city of Harare. I knew about Chikurubi. Even by African standards, Chikurubi is bad. In fact, it has been declared one of the worst prisons in the world by various international human rights organizations. The survival rate back then was ten percent: out of every 100 people who entered those doors, only ten left them alive.

Though I was a prisoner of war, I was not in a POW camp. I was not with other military and certainly not with my own people. In fact, when I arrived at Chikurubi, I learned that I was a rare white guy amongst about 2,000 black guards and approximately 5,000 black prisoners. The other prisoners ran the gamut from political prisoners, petty thieves and innocent men picked up for talking negatively about their government in a bar, to murderers, rapists, and psychopaths. To me, the whole place represented the enemy, regardless of my fellow prisoners' backgrounds. To them, I represented everything wrong, hateful, and bad in Africa: not only was I a white South African, not only was I Afrikaner, but I was Special Forces, and we had a bad-ass reputation in Africa. So while the survival rate for the rest of the Chikurubi population was ten percent, the prognosis for me was zero percent.

When you arrive at Chikurubi, they strip you naked. They take away your possessions, your clothes, your humanity, your dignity and very, very slowly... your life.

I was issued a pair of khaki shorts, a short-sleeved khaki shirt, and three blankets. Those were my sole possessions for the next twelve years and eight months.

Now, when I tell you that for more than a decade, my only possessions were one pair of shorts, one short-sleeved shirt, and three dirty blankets, your mind can't really process what I'm saying because you assume I'm leaving out the obvious—that I had a bed, sheets, soap, socks, toothpaste, comb, underwear. . .

No.

For twelve years, eight months, I had three filthy, lice-infested blankets, one pair of shorts, and one short-sleeved shirt. Nothing else. Not even a scrap of toilet paper.

Being SA Special Forces, I was considered a high-security prisoner because the officials feared a rescue attempt. We were constantly springing our guys and I myself had been captured in the process of doing just that, so it was known that a rescue attempt would be made for me. That gave me great comfort; even though Chikurubi was a nightmare, I figured I wouldn't be there more than a few months.

It also meant, however, that I was placed in the maximum security part of the prison. Those of us in that area were not allowed to wear the shorts and shirt in the prison cell, as it was thought that keeping us naked would be a deterrent to escape. It was also yet another degrading, calculated tactic to dehumanize us. The blankets were thrown in at night and hauled out in the morning.

I shared a cell that measured six by eight meters, or 18 by 24 feet, with 49 other prisoners, sometimes more, oftentimes a few less, depending on how many had died over a few days' time. Sometimes days would go by and we'd have three, four dead bodies lying amongst us that wouldn't be carried out until they began to smell.

It was so crowded in that cell that we had to sleep in two shifts. Those of us getting the first shift had to lie on our sides with our knees drawn up, all of us lined up and pressed together like sardines. It was so tight, I could count the lice crawling through the hair of the prisoner in front of me. The other half of the inmates would sit with their backs against the opposite wall with their knees drawn up, hugged to their chests. Half-way through the night, we'd swap so everybody got a chance to at least lie down, if not sleep.

For most of my prison sentence, I was locked up 24 hours a day, seven days a week with around 49 men in a cell that was built to house 12. There were no windows to the outside. This, combined with the fact that the light burned 24/7, was one of the ways they messed with our minds—we never knew what time it was, or even what day. The only way I knew it was "nighttime" was when the door opened and 150 dirty, crusty, lice-infested blankets were thrown into the cell. It wasn't always technically nighttime. They changed the times they threw in the blankets as yet one more way to keep us disoriented. After just a short while, it became impossible to keep track of time.

About 18 hours out of every 24, the cell buzzed non-stop with the booming voices of my cell mates loudly communicating with—or, more accurately, yelling at—each other in more than a dozen different black dialects.

In black African cultures, it's important to talk loudly. If you speak quietly, it is believed you are gossiping, plotting or, worse, casting a spell. Witchcraft, curses, and spells are an integral part of the tribal culture and are fiercely believed in, even by guys who have left and been educated at places like Oxford or Harvard before coming back to the Continent.

Once one of my cell mates, Shawn, discovered amongst his blankets a pouch filled with dead, dried pieces of bugs, a common combination believed to contain black magic powers that bewitched the receiver. Other cell mates or guards who had an issue with him had planted it in his blanket. Even though Shawn was educated, he was certain he had been bewitched and thus was going to die. No matter how hard I tried to convince him otherwise, within weeks he had fulfilled his own prophesy and was dead.

I was allowed no contact with the outside world: no phone calls, no attorney, no visits, no magazines, books or newspapers, no letters. Although I was with dozens, hundreds, thousands of other people, I felt completely isolated and cut off from the world.

We were fed once a day on a half cup of rice and a half cup of cabbage leaves. The cabbage leaves portion was more like one cabbage leaf, floating in a thin liquid. Ever-present hunger gnawed at me. I became obsessed with food and my lack of it.

The toilet in our cell was a hole in the corner of the room. It had no seat. It was just an open pit. It could not flush, as it had no running water.

I don't know if you've ever been in a room with 50 people using a hole 24/7 as a toilet that cannot be flushed or be cleaned. It stinks.

We got running water once a month for two hours. For this, we were allowed to go outside, hundreds of walking skeletons grasping at thin trickles of water, torn between using the ration to clean some of the caked filth off our bodies or simply sucking down the cool liquid. This was the only moment of refreshment in hundreds of hours of stench and staleness.

As part of our "punishment," the guards would come most mornings and, starting at one side of the prison, using wooden clubs the size of baseball bats, would move from cell to cell, beating their way through the prison until everybody received his beating for the day. In this sense, there was no discrimination in Chikurubi; everyone was beaten equally. Over the years, I saw many people die during those beatings.

In addition to the routine daily group beatings in the cell, I also received private ones. Sometimes I would be handcuffed to a bar above my head, my body hanging from the ceiling like a kudu carcass. A small group of guards and authorities would go at me with bats and steel pipes, favoring my lower back and kidney area. At first, I would have the energy to kick and give some back, but eventually, I would loose the ability to lift my legs. Hanging, I would twist and turn, futilely still trying to maneuver my body away from their blows. Eventually, my shoulders would dislocate and I would simply hang, an easy target for the continued blows. My tormentors would exhaust themselves and take a break, handing their pipe or bat to reinforcements to take over while they rested. While beating me, the men would snarl at me for being a racist *marungu*—white.

Chikurubi fulfilled its reputation: it was a living hell, rife with filth, terror, severe hunger, sickness, and horror. Violence among inmates was often more vicious than that of the guards against the prisoners. Although the violence was mostly tribal- and turf-related, me being *marungu* certainly drew extra attention from my fellow inmates, and the guards and people in charge had a field day with me. By the end of my time in Chikurubi, all my teeth had been either knocked out or had fallen out, and many bones in my body had been broken at one time or another, in addition to my jaw and my nose, which never healed properly and cause me excruciating headaches and nasal problems to this day.

Human rights do not exist in places like Chikurubi. There is no protection for the prisoners, no medical attention, and no law. While watch-dog organizations like Amnesty International and Red Cross International decry what goes on, their good intentions and activism rarely reach inside.

Given my special status, I was given special treatment: I was tortured mercilessly and endlessly by those in charge, ostensibly to get information out of me. For the occasion, I would be invited to don my clothes and walk with the guards through the prison to secluded torture cells. It was never a good thing to be told to get dressed.

Tactics included my torturers ripping a hole in the bottom of a plastic garbage bag, slipping it over my head and tying it around my neck. With the open end above my head, the authorities would slowly begin filling the bag with water, until I began to drown. I was tied down so I couldn't rip the bag off. This tactic would be repeated over and over again, the panic rising each time, knowing what was coming as the level rose to my chin, me desperately trying to clench my mouth shut and futilely lift my chin, then gasping, trying to fill my lungs with air that I could hold, then water rising over my mouth, me sucking in water, water up to my nose, me snorting and writhing, then water rising over my nose to my bulging eyes, taking me to the point of drowning. At the last minute, as I was flailing and screaming in garbled rage, choking, and drowning, the bag would be dropped with chuckles from my tormentors. The session was over only when I passed out unconscious in my own watery vomit.

Repeated electric shock torture, among other things, has left me with raw nerve endings and a body that twitches most nights as I attempt to sleep. No quality of comfortable bed or soft sheets can soothe the throbbing, jolting pain my body still experiences, years after my release.

The first weeks and months were horrific, but my spirits were bolstered by the knowledge that my buddies were coming. I just had to keep my mouth shut and keep myself alive until they reached me, which was just a matter of time. The code of honor was that we never, ever left a brother in a place like this. As protected and secure as Chikurubi was, there were always ways to break someone out; I'd done it myself numerous times for others. I was also a high-ranking officer—a colonel—and my government always took care of those who had served it so well. The intelligence we carried within us was too precious, classified, and hard-won to be left to rot or tortured out.

But as I sat naked on my haunches for hours on end, my mind numb from pain and the din of a gazillion languages being spoken at top volume, doubt would rise to my consciousness: *They should have gotten to me by now. Do they know I'm here? Do they know I'm still alive, waiting for their rescue?*

A plot began to build in my mind: I needed to get word out. I needed to smuggle letters out to be sure my people knew I was here.

How was I to write letters with no access to pen, paper, envelope, or money to buy the materials, much less a stamp? Prison is like everywhere else in the world: the impossible just takes a little longer... and a bit of bribery.

By then I had forged alliances, if not yet friendships, with a few of my fellow inmates. Most of the inmates were local guys and knew the guards, sometimes were even related to them. They would make a deal with the guards to bring them a pen and a piece of paper. The prisoner would give it to me. I'd write a letter and put any address on it that I could remember or think of, sometimes just the name of a place I'd been, like a hotel, or the name of a newspaper. Then I'd give it back to the prisoner—*with that one meal of the day as payment*—and he would give the letter to the guard. Where it went from there, I had no idea.

Over the course of a few years, I wrote hundreds of letters, each time giving away that one paltry meal a day as payment. After a time, with no response, some of the guys in the cell watching this would say to me in their dialect, "Reon, man. C'mon. Give it up. Just eat and forget about it." This would only cause me to redouble my efforts— writing more letters, eating even less food.

It's true that much of my effort might have been futile. How many of those letters ever *left* the prison, I don't know; likely not many. But I do know of one that reached the outside world. One out of hundreds. Somehow one of those letters ended up with a magazine in South Africa called *Out There*. It's a nature magazine and it doesn't publish letters. But for some reason, it published mine.

Back then, South Africa had a population of about 47 million people. Out of those 47 million people, I don't know how many people ever saw or read that letter, but I know of one person who read it...and did something.

He was a young kid, a college guy, named Phillip-Niel Albertyn. He was a typical Afrikaner, raised on a farm, from a family of no particular influence or stature. He'd never heard of me and certainly didn't know me or my story. Apparently he read the letter, went home, and said to his mother and brothers, "I want to help this soldier in captivity. I want to start a support group." His mom and brothers said, "OK. We're your first supporters and we'll tell the family." They later told me that at the time, they didn't think much would come of it. They figured in a few weeks, he'd forget.

However, Phillip never forgot about me. That young man grew into an adult, got a job, got a busy life, but he never forgot me. That person of "no influence or stature" was instrumental in starting a support group that eventually spanned the world and was lobbying governments all over the globe to put pressure on Zimbabwe to release me and send me home. And yes, he was there in the crowd the day I eventually was released.

Of course, I had no idea about any of this at the time. As far as I knew, it was highly likely my letters weren't even getting beyond the prison walls. But I kept at it.

Writing the letters kept me going, it gave me some purpose and something to focus on, besides surviving each day. But my real hope lay in the rescue that was being planned by my buddies and my country. It was our code of honor and I knew they wouldn't let me down.

A creeping realization began to form within me that I repeatedly swatted to the recesses of my brain. I replaced it with questions: *What is going on? Why haven't they come for me by now? They really should have made the rescue during my transfer to Chikurubi; that was the easiest opportunity.*

And then one day the full realization slammed into my brain: *No one is coming. No rescue attempt is going to be ordered, because my superiors don't want me rescued.*

I realized I'd been caught in the government transition. My own government, on its way out, needed to deny any knowledge of me or my activities.

I then thought back to that final mission with new perspective: the Afrikaner regime had been closing up shop and frantically trying to hide everything that could be potentially embarrassing or dangerous for them when the new government came into power. This practice is nothing new and has been done throughout the ages by countries and governments all over the world. Mine was just one more.

The new government was standing in the wings, waiting for their grand entrance. Nelson Mandela had been released after a 27-year imprisonment and was preparing to step in to lead the new South Africa. What a blessing it was for my country that such a man as he existed at that time. But for the rest of them, on both sides, it was a political game, one elite was being swapped for another, and everybody knew it.

The big boys in the Afrikaner government and military were making preparations for their retirement and were ensuring there would be nothing that could come back to haunt them. They were sending out their minions to clean everything up so they could exit in honor and also be well cared for, of course. The foot soldiers were still being used and lied to and manipulated by them in order to accomplish this. I realized I had been one of those minions all those years. I had been hand-picked to rise through the ranks, my reckless boyhood a supreme attribute in their eyes. I had been hand-picked because I was the best of the best—and dispensable.

I realized then that I wasn't meant to survive the ambush. But since I had, my military superiors and government were going to make sure I wasn't around to tell anyone the things I knew. I suddenly understood, *Those bastards* want *me here, in a place where the chances of a lone white Afrikaner surviving 5,000 enemies is nil.*

If I were around, inquiries by the new government would surely be made about what my orders had been during the war. One way or another, my government was going to get rid of me to be certain I didn't come back and screw up the fanfare of their exit and their fat, happy retirement. I was being abandoned by my own people, by my military, and by the country I had served my entire adult life.

My anger boiled over and I went into a rage that caused even Matuvi, the most psychotic, savage guy in our cell, to cower in the corner. I slammed my fists into the concrete walls, breaking bones in my hands as I cursed and blamed my country, the military, my people, my family, God. I vowed to myself, *I will survive and destroy each and every one of those assholes when I get out.*

After rage, came despair.

——————————

I languished for days, weeks, months. I don't know how long exactly. Time didn't exist anymore. Sometimes I would rally to write more letters. I knew I had to keep going, to keep trying. Upon rousing myself, however, the raging rampage would begin again until I was spent and slumped back into a stupor.

When I wasn't emotionally torturing myself with rabid anger and violent visions of revenge, my tormentors were physically torturing me, the guards were beating me, and my cellmates were harassing me. My world narrowed to a tiny slit of seething hatred and brittle bitterness.

═══════════════

One day during feeding time, Inglovo, the guard patrolling us, hesitated for the briefest moment in front of me, dropped something between my haunches, then walked on. I didn't dare look or even acknowledge that anything had happened, so I continued to stare straight forward and eat without missing a beat. As Inglovo walked out and the door slammed shut, I greedily reached down and discovered an envelope. Inside was one page written in Afrikaans with a red pen. A letter!

I had received my first letter from Phillip and learned that not everyone in the world had forsaken me. My country, my government, my buddies had. But a stranger who'd never heard of me had not. I crumpled forward and wept.

═══════════════

With the arrival of Phillip's first letter, a swift smuggling trade got underway, in addition to letters getting in and out. Inglovo was my main accomplice. When I asked him later why he had taken the risk of giving me the first letter, he told me, "I admired how you never gave up."

Now that I had an actual destination and live person receiving my letters, I also had the ability to make requests of the outside world. One of my first? A Bible. Not because I'd suddenly found God. I was still royally pissed off at Him along with everyone and everything else that had gotten me here and left me to die. I did it because I knew it would piss off the guards who came each morning to beat us.

Several weeks back, prior to the first letter, I had requested a Bible of the authorities, as it's the one thing the world over a prisoner cannot be refused. They refused. Their refusal of such an innocuous thing got my Afrikaner ire up and the moment I had the chance, I was on a new mission: smuggling in Bibles. I hoped it would drive the guards crazy and maybe get a few of them in trouble with their superiors. I also hoped it would confound the authorities, stoke their naturally superstitious natures, and generate some paranoia. Hey, I had nothing else to do. And when there's a group of people who holds all the power and inflicts a lot of pain, it's human nature to begin to look for ways to irritate that hateful group of people.

Something interesting happened with those Bibles. After about six months of the first one arriving, the ink on its pages started to disappear. What was going on? It was a rare piece of reading material being passed amongst thousands of people locked up 24 hours a day with lights burning 24/7.

Phillip was thrilled to get the request for the Bibles, as he is a very Christian young man. I felt a little badly letting him think that I was perhaps now a Soldier of the Lord, but I guess not that badly, because I kept at it and, in just a few years, ended up smuggling over 300 Bibles into that place.

It accomplished my goal: the guards would go nuts every time they found that a Bible had somehow mystically appeared amongst dozens of naked guys locked up 24-hours a day. Several of the guards got in trouble for it. Of course, I paid for it, too, but it was worth it.

Bible smuggling accomplished something else that I hadn't been trying to achieve—I read the Bible cover to cover. A few times over. And it got me thinking.

Sometime after the first letter arrived from Phillip, I got extremely ill and needed to see a doctor. Now, in Chikurubi, there's no medical care. There's no medication and there are no doctors. If you get sick, you get better...or you die. I saw many, many people die due to lack of simple medical care, like an antibiotic or even a malaria tablet.

When Phillip and my support group learned that I was ill, they started lobbying the South African government to lobby the Zimbabwean government for some medical care. Months, maybe a year, of politics ensued. Eventually a doctor was allowed to examine me. Upon examining me, he diagnosed prostate cancer and ordered an immediate operation.

If you think I was angry about being sold out, captured, and locked up in that hellhole for 26 years, imagine my fury at finding out that now I had cancer! I cursed everyone all over again. Why me? What had I done that was so much worse than anyone else that I had ended up like this? I was just a soldier serving my country. Why was I paying for the whole world's sins?

At Chikurubi, nobody ever saw a doctor, much less went for an operation. But again, through my support group and months and months of pressure from the international community, I was finally granted permission to go for an operation—on the condition that I pay for it. My support group then had to spend several more months fundraising for me, as I had no other means to pay; my half-cup of rice and half-cup of cabbage weren't going to get me far with a doctor.

Because I was supposedly a high-security prisoner (even though I had given up on my countrymen rescuing me, apparently Zimbabwe hadn't), taking me out of the prison for an operation was a matter of high military security. It was also just one more way to humiliate and dehumanize me. First, I was put in handcuffs and leg irons. Then a chain was wrapped around my waist and padlocked. The other end of the chain was put around a guard and padlocked. I was then surrounded by dozens of guards with AK-47 machine guns, put in the middle of a military convoy and, with choppers flying, outriders roaring, and sirens blaring, was sped off to the hospital in Harare, a major, overblown show-of-might production. "TIA—This is Africa," as the saying goes.

When we got to the hospital, more drama ensued—the Zim soldiers surrounded the hospital and removed the civilian population, who stood outside, their hospital gowns flapping in the wind, wondering who the VIP patient was.

I was placed on a stained, limping gurney and accompanied into the operating room by armed soldiers, who remained in the room to "guard me," their dirty boots clomping on the floor as they walked around, talking loudly and smoking. The chains were not allowed to be removed until I was on the operating theatre table under sedation.

When I woke up, I was back in chains, chained to the guard, in the back of an open pick-up truck in the middle of a convoy on my way back to prison, where they would put me with my 49 fellow prisoners.

Over the years, as the sickness spread, I went for numerous such operations. I never really got better after them and I sometimes wonder if the operations were as bad—or maybe worse—for me than the illness.

I became sicker and weaker. The torture, beatings, malnourishment, squalid conditions, and now cancer, were taking their toll. There were times when I didn't move for days on end, but rather would just sit there on my haunches in my patch of the cell, my mind and spirit far away from the place where my body was imprisoned.

Many nights, I could hear the melancholy hooting of a group of barn owls that had taken up residency outside the prison. These owls live all over Africa and have very distinctive hunting and mating calls that I grew up hearing. As a child, when I heard the owls, I'd walk outside to find them. Lying in my cell, I first identified a male, then a female. Months later, I could identify the calls of their young. It gave me comfort to hear their lonely, nostalgic hooting and I often envisioned myself outside with them, soaring through the night sky.

One night, their beautiful calls ceased. Owls are believed to be witches in black African culture, so the guards had killed them.

After my seventh operation, the doctor finally gave up. "Reon, there's nothing more we can do for you medically," he told me. "You've got six months to live." The cancer had won.

I rallied enough to be stunned and despondent and wonder to myself, *What kind of God makes me go through more than twelve years of this hell, of torture and starvation and filth and terror, and then kills me? Why didn't He kill me in the first place? What is the point of any of this?*

Days later, I was lying in a fetal position in my spot in the cell, an infection festering at the site where I had been operated on. I weighed 48 kilograms, or about 100 pounds, and didn't have a tooth in my mouth. I was dying and I knew it. I doubted I would last the six months I'd been given to live.

Several guards appeared earlier than usual, unlocked the prison door, and said, "Reon, get dressed." I couldn't believe it.

Some political bigwig must be in town, I thought, *and I'm being dragged out as usual as the trophy Afrikaner prisoner to be tortured for "information," twelve years after the fact.*

I knew if they tortured or beat me that day, I wouldn't make it.

I was too weak to get dressed, so the guards helped me. "Where are we going?" I asked repeatedly and they simply said, "Just get dressed and come with us."

The guards escorted me down the stairs to the reception of the prison and I walked into a wall of cameras and a crowd of people yelling at me in excited voices that I couldn't understand at first, it had been so long since I had heard Afrikaans spoken. The camera flashes hurt my eyes and the people across the room were a blurry haze that I couldn't make out. For more than a decade, I hadn't seen anything further than eight meters in front of my face and my eyesight had suffered for it. The noise, the light, the jostling crowd of mostly white people shoving microphones in my face unnerved me. *What is all this about?*

Suddenly, one voice cut through to my brain and I heard, "Reon, what does it feel like to be pardoned and going home?"

I was stunned. There had been no discussion of my release, only of my impending death. There had been no warning that this day was coming. I stood in a daze, my mind racing, and I thought, *Is this a joke? Is this really happening?*

Zimbabwean president Robert Mugabe had always vowed that I would die in his prison. *Mugabe is so close to getting his wish. What is going on?* I wondered. *What kind of trap is this now?*

A man stepped forward and introduced himself to me as an MP, a member of the South African parliament. He had been working with my support group to lobby the Zimbabwean government for my release. It was true, he assured me. I had been pardoned and was being released.

I had made it. I was going home!

When I left South Africa in 1990 and crossed that border into Zimbabwe, there had been no cell phones. There had been no laptops. There had been no Internet. I had been put on ice for almost 13 years and then, just like that, I was told, "You're a free man" in front of the international press corps. There I was, suddenly out in the world again.

As I faced the flurry of world media, I tried to process what was happening to me. The MP tapped me on the shoulder and said, "Reon, somebody wants to speak to you," and he handed me what looked like a space-age walkie-talkie.

I took the contraption and, trying to appear intelligent in front of all that media, stared thoughtfully at it, as if pondering what to say, when in fact I was trying to figure out what to *do* with the thing. Guys in and out of prison had told me about something called cell phones, so I figured that's what it was. The MP said, "Reon, speak. They're waiting." I held the thing in front of my mouth like a two-way radio and said, "Hello. Come in. Over," then put it up to my ear to hear a response. The crowd laughed in warm glee and more cameras flashed, trying to catch the skinny, long-lost, and dazed South African "spy" doing a funny trick. They weren't being malicious; it was just that I was such a phenomenon—not only had one of the last white South African soldiers in captivity just been released, I had survived the notorious Chikurubi Prison. I was a curiosity and they wanted to capture it all on film.

I was flown to South Africa in a military jet. At the press event at Johannesburg International Airport, I learned that most of my family had died while I was in prison. They never knew I was alive; they had been told I was killed in combat. My little sister, Byrene, was left, but I hadn't seen her in more than 20 years, so she was a stranger to me.

I was also told, in essence, by the new government, "You didn't work for us. You worked for the Apartheid regime. And you're going back on trial as a war criminal."

I had made it. My dream had come true. I was home...in a country that didn't want me, with no job, no money, no possessions, no family, no friends, no education, and terminally ill.

I had made it.

For what?

_____

The South African government detained me for six weeks for a standard debriefing in regard to my POW experience. Concurrently, it was determined there were no criminal charges against me and thus I would not go on trial. I was given the "option," however, of appearing before the Truth and Reconciliation Committee (TRC). I simply had to report everything I'd ever done for the old government—including providing the names and ranks of anyone else involved in any mission I had ever done over my 18-year career—and I'd be retired with honor, full rank, and full pension, including medical aid. My 152 months in Chikurubi would be counted as "active duty," and my pension would be all that much larger because of it.

Here was my first opportunity to get my revenge on all those who had sold me out and left me to rot. More than that, it solved my employment challenge and my health-care problems. I readied myself for my appearance before the Commission.

In the meantime, I had become a national and even international celebrity of sorts. Major news organizations conducted interviews with me. People sent me gifts. A few sent me hate mail. A dentist who saw me on the news gave me the gift of a full set of dentures to fill my empty mouth. Everywhere I went in my country, people came up to me and shook my hand saying, "Welcome home, Brother." The vast majority of those people were blacks.

Most whites, on the other hand, kept a cautious distance.

The media and acquaintances kept asking me, "What are you going to do now that you're a free man?" My dazed response was along the lines of, "I don't know." More than one person said, "You suffered so much, man. You should just go sit on the beach and chill out." What they didn't say, but I heard very clearly was, "...and die."

As the time neared for my appearance before the TRC, I began to feel great unease. As I reviewed those I was about to implicate, it struck me what was bothering me: I wasn't just impacting a few dozen people. I would be impacting hundreds. Most of those guys had not gone to the TRC, but instead had faded away to farm. They had moved on with their lives and put the hell of the war behind them, if they could. They now had families—wives and children. How many lives would I ruin to get what I needed?

I did not appear before the TRC.

I was stripped of my rank, my honor, and my pension.

═══════════

I drifted through the next days. My support group continually provided a feast, but I couldn't eat much. I couldn't really bear to watch them eat either. So much food seemed an unnecessary extravagance. In the evenings, I opted to sleep on the floor, next to the nice bed in the little farm house my support group had arranged for me. Sleep rarely came and when it did, it quickly transformed into nightmares. I stalked the halls through the night and into the wee hours of dawn. I watched the sunrise and walked barefoot on the grass, filled with a mixture of gratitude and sorrow. *I am out of Chikurubi...but will I ever be able to be back in society?* I wondered.

And continually running through my mind was, *Why? Why has all this happened to me? What has been the point? Is there really no meaning to any of it and will my life end with me dying alone and impoverished?*

PART II:

FREEDOM

INTRODUCTION—PART 2

Emancipate yourself from mental slavery,
none but ourselves can free our minds.
—Bob Marley

A lthough my story sounds like a sad one, a "poor me," hard luck saga, it's not.

This is a happy story and I am the most blessed man who walks this earth. Today as I write this, I have no hatred, no bitterness, no anger, and no regrets about what happened to me in my life because I have come to realize that everything that did happen—the good and the bad—all had a purpose. I transformed in Chikurubi through lessons I would never have been able to learn anywhere else, in any other way. And as the years since my release have gone on, I have found that the lessons I learned were not meant just for me. Hundreds of thousands of people have come to hear my story and its lessons. I cannot tell you what my story does for people because I don't know. It's just my story. But I *can* tell you it changes people.

Hearing what I went through and how I have used the experience to transform the way I live appears to help others, and it brings me great joy to be of such service in the world. But I've also felt great sadness as I've traveled the globe sharing my story, because I've met so many people living in prisons far worse than Chikurubi.

These are prisons created and built by themselves in their own heads, hearts, and minds. And the sad thing is, they don't even realize they've imprisoned themselves and that they are their own guards. They are awesome people with beautiful lives but they've imprisoned themselves with their egos, their money, their fears, their possessions, their status, unhappy careers, bad relationships, blame, anger, resentment, hatred, some incident that happened 20 years ago in their life, or an injustice done to them yesterday. People hang onto these things as if keeping them alive serves them. In fact, such negativity is killing them.

If I had to choose between a prison like that and Chikurubi, I'd go back to Chikurubi.

One of the hardest things to do is to look at oneself honestly and clinically. I've found that very few people are willing to look closely at who they are, because they don't like themselves very much. Many people are unhappy with their lives. Usually, they blame people and factors outside themselves for that unhappiness.

I say: if you're unhappy, the power and the responsibility to change that lies with you. Even in the most impossible situations, change is possible. The choice is yours. If something bothers you, do something about it, or be quiet. If there's nothing that you can do about it, then accept it and work within it. Believe me, even when there's no way out, there is always a way through.

Most importantly, forgive others; forgive yourself.

If you don't like your life, if you don't feel happiness, you might need to question some of the things you've been conditioned to believe, then work to reprogram your mind to change those ingrained attitudes. From there, you can start experiencing peace and happiness, no matter what is happening around you. That is not to say that you will go through life laughing and smiling all the time. But it will give you the ability to cope with life's ups and downs, which is really a more useful tool. Maggie and I talk about this more in The 10 Principles that follow.

Life is not perfect. Bad things happen and I'm sorry about that. But you do have a choice even then: you may not always be able to choose what happens to you, but you *can* choose how you respond to what happens to you. If you forget everything else I say, remember that.

What I tell you may be simple, but it's not necessarily easy. I know that. I spent 12 years, eight months, struggling to remember that I could choose my response, that I had the power to choose my experience based on my attitude. I still have to choose every moment how I will go through my day.

I don't have a secret to sell. I can't give you the answers. I can't give you a formula. What I can give you is an example. I am living proof of what I say and of what is possible. What I can tell you is that by putting into practice what I came to realize, I no longer experience anger, bitterness, or hatred. I still have hassles every day, and yet I am at total and utter peace and experience happiness, regardless of what is going on around me.

The lessons I've learned are not new. In fact, they're age old. But perhaps set in the unfamiliar context of my experience, they might spark a new understanding in you. Everything I tell you, you already know. But sometimes you need a reminder.

It is said that a fool learns from his own mistakes, but a wise man learns from a fool's mistakes. You choose.

THE 10 PRINCIPLES
TO SET YOURSELF FREE

1st Principle:
FORGIVE

*Resentment is like drinking poison
and then hoping it will kill your enemies.*
—Nelson Mandela

Through my experience, I learned that forgiveness is not what many of us think it is. We think we have to be some great and very holy person to be "big enough" to forgive.

Forgiveness is not for others; it's for ourselves. It's not something we give to others; it's something we do for ourselves.

When those guards came in the mornings to beat us, I wanted to kill them. I hated them with everything in me. But not just them. I hated everyone. For years in Chikurubi, I was obsessed with thoughts about the various methods of revenge I would exact on my torturers, the guards, the other prisoners who beat me, and on my military superiors and colleagues who had abandoned me. I was a bitter, angry, hate-filled man.

After a few years, however, I realized that my hatred of those people wasn't doing *them* any harm. It wasn't affecting *their* lives. I was wasting untold amounts of precious energy on the very people I hated. And it made no difference. The world kept going on; I kept getting beaten and tortured, our conditions were still squalid, I was still in prison. My anger wasn't changing anything, affecting anyone, bothering anyone, or making a difference to anybody. But it *was* destroying me. It was blinding me, paralyzing me and eating me alive. Nothing I could do would hurt the people I hated in the way I wanted to hurt them in order to get the satisfaction and relief I needed. So I had to find a different avenue for relief. Forgiveness was that avenue.

The first person I forgave was myself.

I believe to forgive others, you must first examine what role you had in the situation and accept responsibility. It is rare that you have had no role in what has happened to you in your life. Look closely and with humility. This is a heavy thing to do and can be scary. Our egos are programmed to fight us tooth and nail on accepting any personal responsibility. It seems like it's much easier to blame others—and from there, to be angry at them and hate them—than it is to take responsibility.

But I came to realize that I was paying a heavy toll for my blame of others: as long as I blamed others, I was trapped in anger.

I also started to realize that blaming and hating everyone else was in part an excuse my mind had made up so I didn't have to take responsibility for anything wrong I had done in *my* life. But if I was really honest: whose fault was it that I was in Chikurubi? No one had forced me to become Special Forces. No one had held a gun to my head to cross that border into Zimbabwe. I had chosen those things.

Accepting responsibility for my life was overwhelming. It was like scales falling from my eyes: I suddenly saw everything and everyone— myself included—for what and who they really were. My heroes melted into mere humans, and flawed ones at that. Everything I believed in and had been taught came into question. I felt lost at sea. A huge weight descended upon me. It was devastating to realize what I had been responsible for creating in the past.

But then a surprising thing happened: as I took responsibility for my life, I began to have a sense of power in it, even in Chikurubi. Because if I was taking responsibility for my life in the past and responsibility for what I had created in the past, couldn't I also take responsibility for what I wanted to create going forward? If I had chosen my actions in the past, couldn't I choose my future actions?

This realization filled me with the redemptive grace needed to forgive myself for the past and to accept the responsibility that I had the power to choose my life going forward.

The next task was to forgive all those who had wronged me, chief among them those who had abandoned me and those who were abusing me. Having accepted responsibility for my own life, however, I realized I also had the ability to choose to forgive others; I had the power to choose to stop wasting my energy on my enemies. But how? And then it hit me: I was giving *up* my power by hating them. I was *allowing* them to hold me mentally, emotionally and spiritually captive through my hatred, resentment and anger. Forgiving *them* set *me* free. This realization unlocked it for me. Forgiveness of even the most heinous actions suddenly became possible. I was motivated to forgive everyone, so I could free myself from their emotional clutches. I will never again be anyone's prisoner, in any way, shape, or form.

Forgiveness is an ongoing practice. Perhaps you can just say, "I forgive you" and never think of the incident again. For me it wasn't so simple. It's easy to say, "I forgive." What's difficult is to make the internal switch to let it go. Hatred is ingrained through practice, just as forgiveness is, and is thus hard to break. I had to catch myself every time my mind went to hatred, anger or blame of my enemies or something that had happened, stop the thought and replace it with thoughts like, "I do not give you my power or energy anymore. I forgive you." I had to continually, consciously choose forgiveness, until I had neutralized the feelings of hatred and anger.

The more I forgave, the easier it became, and the freer I felt.

EXERCISE: Forgive

Reon's experience reveals that as long as you feel irritation, resentment, anger or hatred toward someone, as long as thinking about an incident or person riles you up, you are being held prisoner by the very situation or person you hate. As long as you hold a grudge against others, hate them, or refuse to forgive them, you are in their power and they are in charge of your life. They may not even remember you or the incident, they may have moved on, moved away, or even be dead, but you continue to give them the power to hold you emotionally captive. Likewise, you rob yourself of happiness, love and joy by harboring hatred.

Set yourself free right now! Forgive those who have wronged you. Refuse to give them any more "air time" in your head or your heart.

Think of someone who has wronged you or for whom you feel hatred, or recall an incident that really burned you up. What emotions do you feel right now?

Where in your body do you feel these emotions?

How often do you think about this person or the incident?

Ask yourself the following questions:
Is there anything I need to or can do to resolve the situation? If so, what?

Are these steps practical and truly helpful in resolving a situation, or are they vengeful? Vengeance tends to breed more time spent thinking about the person or incident, rather than releasing oneself from it.

What benefit do I derive from continuing to hate this person or feel anger about this incident? Who does this serve? Does it make me a better person, more productive, happier?

How much more time am I willing to be in this person's power or captive to this situation?

Am I ready to let go of this anger or hatred? What will I say to myself every time the thought of this person or this incident comes up in my mind?

It's very important to resist the urge to blame yourself instead of accepting responsibility for your actions and your life. Blaming yourself is a cop-out and yet another trick of the mind to get out of taking responsibility for your actions. If you need to apologize to someone, apologize. If you find yourself wallowing in self-blame, however, recognize it as the negative and self-defeating work of your ego and redirect your thoughts to accepting responsibility, forgiving yourself and staying conscious of your choices going forward. If there truly is no responsibility to accept in a situation, don't make it up. Again, that is a trap.

NOTES

2ND PRINCIPLE:
LOVE AND
SERVE OTHERS

I cried because I had no shoes. Until I saw a man who had no feet.
—**Sa'di**

n *The First Principle: Forgive*, I'm not suggesting that you must always *forget* what happened and I'm certainly not telling you to pretend something didn't happen or to minimize something important that transpired. Sometimes you need to remember an incident or tragedy to keep it from being repeated. But you can remember without feeling hatred or anger and thus without further damaging yourself. *That* is what is freeing.

When something truly tragic has happened—a violent death of a loved one, for instance—holding onto the anger or sorrow can be a shield, or viewed as a way to keep the memory of that person alive. Is it? How does it benefit you or the person who is gone? If justice needs to be served, fight for justice. But do it without anger or it will destroy you.

Do not confuse forgiving with accepting, allowing, or inviting injustice, wrong-doing, or hurtful behavior. You do not have to like what happened, like someone's actions, or even like the person in order to forgive, or even *after* you have forgiven that person.

One morning, I was lying on the cell floor, the guards had just walked out after beating all of us, including one of my buddies who was lying senseless, and I thought to myself, *I don't get this. I really don't. In the Bible God tells me to love my enemy. How can I love these guys? All I want to do is rip their heads off.*

Suddenly something inside of me said to me, "I did not tell you to *like* them. I told you to *love* them."

I wondered, *How would that work?*

As I continued to think about it, however, I came to understand the meaning of the words. I explain it this way: on a simple level, don't we all have someone we just don't like somewhere in our extended families—a great aunt, an uncle, or an in-law? But we love them. They're family. Can't we extend that concept outwards to the rest of the world?

We don't all need to *like* each other or agree with each other. We don't need to like what other people are doing or saying or how they are living their lives. The trick is loving them, *despite* what they are doing or saying. The truth is, however, that we love to make others wrong more than we are willing to simply love them. We spend a whole lot of energy on making others wrong and proving ourselves right.

You can dislike the action, but love the person. Do not confuse the two.

In the process of loving someone even when you don't like that person, you might even find that the differences you assumed were so great, are not so large after all. The guys with whom I became the closest friends in that prison were the ones who had been my worst enemies during the war: the Pan-African National Congress (PAC) and the African National Congress (ANC) guerrillas. A few of them were even guys I had literally shot at, or who had shot at me. As we got to talking, though, we came to realize that we had much in common, and even liked one another. We realized that we might have been friends on the outside if our respective leaders had not told us to shoot at one another.

Always remember that carrying anger, hatred, bigotry, or a grudge actually holds *you* prisoner. Hating a person or a group of people for what they do or believe or how they behave does nothing to hurt them, but much to harm you.

When I realized this and then also got the point about loving others even when I don't *like* what they are doing, I was even able to start viewing the guards as human beings. Believe me, that didn't change how I felt about being beaten. But in opening to the possibility of loving them despite not liking them or their actions, I was able to see beyond their actions and start understanding that they believed they were doing their job. I was able to see how they lived in fear of the authorities and I was even able to feel compassion for their lot in life. I still did not like them or their actions, but I came to understand what "I told you to love them" means.

I meet so many people who tell me things like, "Reon, my daughter and I haven't spoken in ten years." They go on to recount an incident that offended them and caused the rift. When I hear things like this, I am incredulous. How can you not speak to your own child or your own parent? People seem to be loving each other conditionally: "I'll love you as long as you behave the way I want or expect you to." I don't think this is the way we are meant to love each other, especially those most precious in our lives. By carrying such grudges, we are allowing our egos to cut us off from giving and receiving love and support. I repeat: we can dislike the action, but still love the person.

We can also learn to serve others as a way to express our love. I'm not talking about romantic love. I'm talking about love of others as our fellow humans.

After my first operation I was lying on the floor of the cell feeling sorry for myself, wondering, *Why? Why me? Why am I the one who has to go through all this and suffer like this?* when a comic strip I had seen as a kid many, many years ago popped into my head. It was about an old Viking warrior, Hagar the Horrible, who was always in trouble. The comic I remembered was just two little pictures:

In the first one, Hagar is standing on this high mountaintop. It's dark. Rain, hail, snow and thunder are coming down on him. Hagar has his hand stretched up to heaven and is saying, "Why me?"

The second picture is pitch black with a little white bubble coming from Heaven containing just two words, "Why not?"

It was like a light bulb went on in my head. I thought to myself, *That's not a joke. I mean, 'Why not?' What am I actually saying when I say, 'Why me?'*

I suddenly realized that it's actually a very selfish thing to say or think because what "Why me?" implies is, "I'm too good for this pain and sorrow or these problems. Let it happen to the whole world, I don't care, as long as it's not happening to me. "

But when I thought about it, I had to ask myself, *What have I ever done in my life that is so significant that I should be spared?*

And if I wanted to be really honest, there was nobody to blame for me being in Chikurubi other than myself. I chose to become a soldier. Every mission I said yes. The last mission I said yes. I crossed that border willingly. So who was actually responsible for what I was experiencing?

Before you cry, "Why me?" perhaps consider what responsibility you might carry for the situation.

Beyond realizing the responsibility I had in my situation, here I was moaning, "Why me?" when in fact I was one of the *lucky* ones. I had a support group out there lobbying on my behalf, getting me medicine from time to time, and even raising money so I could get an operation. Many of the guys in my cell had no one, or if they did, they couldn't help because they were too poor themselves.

I looked around at my cellmates with new eyes. There was suffering all around me. Yes, I was in bad shape. Yes, I was being singled out for worse treatment than everyone else, but there were guys right next to me in their final days, dying horrible, protracted deaths. There were guys in there who were completely innocent and were locked up with no charge and no sentence. It was then that I started getting interested in my fellow prisoners.

I started sharing my medication when I had some. I started asking my support group to collect extra items for my cellmates. I helped some guys get an attorney. I wrote letters for some who couldn't write. Others I helped to die with dignity. When I started worrying about other people's problems, mine became very insignificant. It taught me that we should be thankful for what we have, rather than always crying about what we don't have or what we want.

That was the moment my life changed. When I began serving others, I had less time to focus on my own woes and complaints. When I began to help others, I found purpose in my day-to-day existence in a place that heretofore had seemed purposeless.

EXERCISE: Love and Serve Others

Reon came to learn that it's possible to hold the duality of not liking someone or that person's actions, but still loving the person. Are you willing to try?

=========

Whom do you dislike or hold a grudge against because you don't agree with that person's or group's beliefs, lifestyle, or actions?

Now consider loving that person or group of people, despite not liking them. What feelings arise in you?

"Serve Others" can be a way of life, not just a special project for an underprivileged group of people. Doing small things for others, such as opening a door for a stranger, bringing your spouse or parent coffee in bed, or picking up a piece of trash in the park, is as much part of the lifestyle of "Serve Others," as building a village in a third-world country. The important factor is not how big, but with what intention you are serving.

Reon points out that a lifestyle of serving others requires you to be conscious of what is going on around you, rather than fully consumed in your own life. It's also a way to stay humble, and thus stay human and compassionate.

In Column 1 of this table, create a list of people (or animals, or organizations, or places) that you recognize as being in need in each of the categories in the far-left column.

	1. Who?	2. Small Service	3. Big Service
My Family			
My Friends			
My Community			
My Work/ school			
My Country			
The World			

Now consider ways, big and small, that you can truly serve those you identified as being in need, and fill in the Small Service (Column 2) and Big Service (Column 3) boxes for each audience. If you are unsure, ask those you would like to serve how you can best serve them.

Truly serving others comes with no strings attached. As you consider who you would like to serve and how, ask yourself: What expectations do I have from this person or people or organization?

Are you still willing to serve, even if you don't receive as much as a "thank you"?

Try not to view serving others as charitable work and instead, stay open to the gifts and understandings you receive from those you are serving. As you do acts of service large and small, reflect here on what you may have learned in the process.

NOTES

3RD PRINCIPLE:
PERSEVERE

Where there's hope, there's life.
It fills us with fresh courage and makes us strong again.
—Anne Frank

A lot of people talk about failure as a learning tool, and I agree. We learn the most through our mistakes; I know I do. Interestingly, the places in life where I might perceive myself to have failed most spectacularly are the times when I learned the most. Young people ask me the best questions and one of them is, "Would you change anything in your life?" No, I wouldn't. Because then I wouldn't be who I am. Of course, I don't want to be involved in war again, I don't want to kill people, and I don't ever want to be in prison again. But without those difficult experiences and the mistakes I made, I wouldn't be who I am.

I have a little bit different take on the subject of failure these days: it simply doesn't exist for me any more because my experiences have taught me that failure can only exist the moment I choose to give up. That thought is so liberating. I never again have to fear failure because failure doesn't exist in my vocabulary any longer. No one and no thing can make me fail.

If you die trying to reach a goal, you have not failed. Failure only becomes a reality the moment you say, "I can't do this. I'm giving up."

While in prison, I wrote hundreds of letters, not knowing if any of them were "succeeding." It sure seemed futile, as nothing happened for a few *years*! My cellmates certainly made me feel like I was failing every time they pointed out I was wasting my time and my precious little food on something that was hopeless. And maybe one could say I did fail hundreds of times to get a letter out.

But from my perspective, I did not fail hundreds of times; I learned hundreds of lessons about how to get a letter out of the prison properly. More than that, I learned that all I needed was one to make it out in order to succeed. Most of all, I learned that the only way I could fail was to give up. If nothing had happened for twenty years, I still wouldn't have failed. If I had died trying I still wouldn't have failed. The only way I could have failed was by saying, "I give up."

The problem is not failure; it's that we psyche ourselves out. That's because we live in what I call an "instant pudding" world: we want everything quick, fast, and easy. If something doesn't come instantly or easily, we say it's not working, it's failed, we've failed. But actually, what happens next is what causes us to fail: we say, "I give up." We have to believe in what we are doing in order to succeed, because that's what keeps us going when it's not "instant pudding" success.

Something even more defeating than expecting instant pudding success is giving up before you've even tried. "It's hopeless." "It will never work." "I can't do that." If that's what you think, you're right. It will never work. Imagine if I had *thought about* writing letters, but had said, "Oh, well. I'm naked and have nothing to write with so that's hopeless. That will never work. I can't do that." I'd likely still be sitting in Chikurubi, with twenty years behind me and another six years left to go in my sentence.

You cannot succeed if you do not try or take action. It's a pretty simple law of the Universe. And if you're going to try, then try your *best*.

In life, there will always be the detractors and naysayers, those people who tell you it can't be done. "You can't do that!" "That's impossible." If I had listened to all the people in my life who told me something couldn't be done, I'd probably still be hunting for scrap metal in Brakpan, South Africa.

Do you know how many times I wanted to give up in Chikurubi? Many, many, many times. Sometimes it felt like it would be the more sane, merciful thing to do for myself. But imagine if the morning I was lying there dying on the floor of my cell and I had given up? If I had said, "I can't do it anymore. I give up." And then five minutes later, the guards had come to tell me to get dressed. I had no idea that my release was coming. I might have given up just moments shy of reaching the goal.

What if, when I had returned to South Africa, I had accepted defeat and decided to go live on a beach and wait to die as many people had suggested I do? What if I had said, "I give up. This is too much." I would never have shared my story and would never have known that I had something to give this world.

My point is this: we don't know the moment our success is coming or who might be working on our behalf out there to help us make it happen. We don't know how formed our success already is.

Are you willing to give up, knowing that what you've worked for might be just moments away from arriving?

I know it gets tough. Believe me, I know it gets discouraging to feel like you're getting nowhere, that you're not making progress no matter how hard you try. But I'm here to tell you that as dark as things might get at times, as tough as the going may get, hang on. The "door" could open for you tomorrow. But if you give up today, you'll never know how close you were.

I am also living proof that *everything passes*—the good and the bad. Nothing lasts forever. When you feel you can't hang on, hang on just another moment. That's how I got through the worst periods. *Everything passes.* I wanted to die so many times during the torture. But you know what? Even those most hellish times had an ending to them. *Everything passes.*

No one can make you fail. No one can make you give up. Only you get to choose to give up.

Sometimes things change in your life and maybe you're not as passionate about what you were pursuing. Or what you're doing does not make sense any longer, so you try a different tack or let it go altogether. That's not failure. That's just common sense.

I find it curious when people tell me they are trying to accomplish thus and such...but are not taking any steps, or enough steps, to further their goal. They are playing a trick on themselves, which is probably the number one way people create failure for themselves. They may be very busy--talking about their goals, thinking about their goals, planning for their goals to be achieved—but are they busy working toward their goal, taking practical action? Oftentimes not.

Let me illustrate what I mean, again using the letters. Suppose I had sent one letter or maybe ten, and then I had decided to wait the next few months to see if I received a response. Or suppose I had decided to pray or send out good intentions that someone would realize I was socked away in a Zimbabwean prison, instead of writing letters. When nothing happened, I could have said, "I failed." "That didn't work." "I must not be intending right." "God didn't hear me." "Well, I tried."

The door opening for me was not just pure dumb luck, or simply a survival contest. The door opened through a combination of God's grace, good luck, outside help, and helping myself. I always say, "Yes. Get on your knees and pray...and then get up off your knees and do something to help yourself!" I spent those years writing hundreds of letters, lobbying any government that would listen, working to keep my thoughts and attitude from killing me, not sitting idly by, wringing my hands, wishing to get out of there and wondering if I would ever be released.

The realization that no one was coming for me was a big one. I had been waiting for others to save me. When they didn't do as I had expected, I was disappointed, to put it mildly.

Expectations of others and disappointment in them because you perceive they are not doing enough to help you are the twin evils that distract you from creating your own success. How many times do you wait for someone else to make you successful, to make "it" happen for you? No one can *make* you happy. And no one can *make* you successful, just as no one can *make* you give up. "God helps those who help themselves," as the saying goes. If you want something badly enough, help yourself to reach the goal. The irony is, once you commit to helping yourself, angels will appear along the way to assist you.

EXERCISE: Persevere

What if failure no longer existed in your reality unless you chose it?

Success is as simple as sticking with a goal until it comes to fruition. So many people want a magic formula. They even want to imbue Reon with superhuman powers to explain why he succeeds at life. But as Reon points out, it's not magic—it's perseverance! There are other factors involved: God's grace, the help of others, a seemingly lucky break. Yet simply waiting for intervention is not the answer; you need to take steps to move yourself closer to your goal, and if you really want it, you need to keep going until you reach it.

Most of us give up way too quickly and don't recognize this as a lack of perseverance. We always have a choice: to give up or to give it our all.

Make a list of what you would you attempt if there were no failure.

Go back and star those items you would like to pursue.

Write down a past "failure" or "failures."

Look deeper. Can you identify a moment or moments when you chose to give up?

Look again at those perceived "failures" and identify what lesson(s) might have been learned.

Which goal or goals did you give up on too quickly?

How are you in charge of whether you succeed or fail?

Now write down a goal you achieved. What were the points when you wanted to, or almost did, give up, but kept going? How did you keep going? Remember those "keep going" moments the next time you hit a roadblock.

Go back to your starred goals. What steps will you take to further you along the path to your goal or goals?

Check in with yourself: Are you expecting "instant-pudding" success?

What roadblocks might arise? Brainstorm some possible solutions.

Ask yourself: Do I want this goal enough that I will choose to keep going when these roadblocks arise?

NOTES

4TH PRINCIPLE: ACCEPT YOUR CIRCUMSTANCES

Acceptance of what has happened is the first step
to overcoming the consequences of any misfortune.
—William James

Sometimes in life, you find yourself in circumstances you don't like or want or didn't consciously choose.

Through my experiences, I discovered that before you can change a situation, you have to first acknowledge and accept that you're even in the situation or set of circumstances in the first place. And when I say accept it, I really mean *accept* it. A lot of times, people say, "Yes, I accept that this is my situation," but they really haven't accepted it. How do I know?

As long as you are still constantly thinking about a situation, as long as you are griping about it or telling the story of your circumstances to try to explain to others why it's wrong or difficult, as long as there's someone or something you are blaming for the situation, as long as there is still emotion and charge around a situation for you, and especially if there's a "but" after, "Yes, I have accepted my situation," it's a dead giveaway that you have not truly accepted your situation.

Many times, we will not acknowledge or accept our situation because we do not want to look at ourselves honestly and clinically. We delude ourselves into thinking it is easier to blame someone or something else than it is to accept our situation, or we tell ourselves that we are not who we really are or that we are not in the situation we truly are in. When stated so simply, it sounds like madness.

It is only when you have really, truly accepted the reality of your circumstances that you can identify action steps that fit the reality of the situation, and then begin to change it.

For the first few years in Chikurubi, I could not truly accept the reality that I was there. Of course, intellectually, I knew I was there. But it's not what I wanted for my life, so I could not accept that Chikurubi was my reality. I was furious that I was there and blamed everyone.

Furthermore, I refused to acknowledge that no one was coming to save me. In my mind, Chikurubi was a temporary situation until my buddies came to rescue me.

While such denial might be a helpful coping mechanism for a short period, and perhaps such fantasy kept me alive initially, it was not a productive long-term strategy, because, oddly enough, as long as I was in non-acceptance of my situation, I was stuck in it. I was kept from moving forward and taking measures to deal with it. Non-acceptance kept me in limbo.

This may seem to fly in the face of those who tell you to keep a positive attitude. Accepting reality is not the same as giving up hope. I'm not suggesting you not have a positive attitude or that you not keep hope alive; I'm suggesting that you have a *realistic* attitude so you can take concrete action to resolve the situation. Whether you choose to have a positive or negative realistic attitude is up to you.

Once I acknowledged that no one was coming to break me out and I faced reality and accepted the fact that I was in Chikurubi, looking at a 26-year sentence, my initial response was, of course, despondence. But then something else began to take hold: a sense of purpose. If this was reality, then I needed to figure out how I was going to survive the situation. Once I accepted my reality, I could then examine my circumstances from a fresh perspective and figure out what I needed to do to survive. Interestingly, I started to see many options and choices within a situation that just moments prior had seemed to have no choices. It taught me that, until I acknowledge and accept my situation, other options or possibilities are not available to me.

Resistance to the situation kept me imprisoned in it. How do you accept your situation? I recommend you start with the facts. Let me give you an example.

For the first three or four years of my sentence, I was constantly hungry. All day long, all I could think about was food. "I'm starving to death," "I need more food," "I can't live on this," were the extent of my thoughts. One day I had a new thought, *I can't go another twenty years or so being obsessed with food and starving. I've got to do something different.*

I decided to examine the facts and the facts were: it had been three or four years living on that little bit of food and I was still alive. I wasn't feeling good, I certainly wasn't looking good, but I was still alive. So the fact was, that little bit of food was indeed enough to sustain my life.

The problem was, I did not want to *acknowledge* that it was enough to sustain my life. I was resisting that reality. I grew up being taught that I needed three meals a day to survive—preferably large, home-cooked ones—so my belief system was keeping me in denial that a lousy half-cup of rice and a half-cup of cabbage leaves was enough to live on.

I also did not want to *accept* that that small bit of food was enough to sustain me because it was not what I wanted. I wanted plates full of delicious Afrikaner meats and mashed potatoes.

But as long as I would neither acknowledge nor accept my situation, I was holding myself hostage to it because I couldn't think beyond it to do anything differently or to find a creative solution. There was no solution as far as I could see because I didn't want to be in the situation in the first place.

An idea kept gnawing at my brain that I couldn't quite reach. One day it struck me: *The facts prove that this food is enough to sustain my life. So it's not the food that's the problem. It's not the amount of food or the quality of food or the number of times a day that I receive it. I'm the problem because I don't want to accept this situation.*

You see, blame is where our mind goes to when we refuse to accept our situation—we blame someone else for us being there, causing it, creating it, or we blame the situation itself. While we are so busy blaming, we are in denial and there is no room for solutions.

As I began to accept and acknowledge that the food was enough to sustain me, another thought came to me: *If I can't change the food, if I can't steal more, buy more or beg more—what* can *I change?*

Me!

The truth is, the only thing we have control over is ourselves. We are the key, the "Determining Factor," in every situation or circumstance in our lives.

I decided to try an experiment. Every time I thought of food or how hungry I was, I'd tell myself, "I'm not hungry."

I must have told myself that a gazillion times a day. "I'm not hungry." I even argued with myself. But I kept at it. I had nothing else to do! Over time, it became a mantra. I don't know how long I said that refrain to myself, but it was a long, long time. Probably several months.

One day I was sitting in my usual cross-legged position in my usual patch of space in the cell and I realized something had changed. I couldn't put my finger on it—I was still in prison, the cell was still overcrowded, noisy and filthy, the beatings were still happening every day, but something had changed. And then I realized: *I haven't been hungry or obsessed about food for a long, long time.*

I was stunned. I had actually reprogrammed my mind. Nothing else had changed but my attitude, and that had changed my experience completely. I realized: *They may have my body, but they do not have my mind and my soul and, therefore, I am still free.*

I would not have been able to reach this understanding if I had continued to refuse to acknowledge and accept my circumstances. I would not have been able to reprogram my conditioned mind if I had remained resistant to the situation.

Before change can happen, we must accept our circumstances.

Something I see very often is people not only not accepting their circumstances, but not accepting the reality of the people in their lives. This lack of acceptance creates tremendous annoyance: the other person is continually letting them down, surprising them with his or her behavior, or irritating them with actions, behaviors, fetishes, or habits. This has to do with *expectations*.

When you have expectations of someone that do not match who that person is, it creates disappointment and very often blame. But who is really to "blame"? The person holding the expectation that doesn't match reality, not the "offending" person!

Since "coming back to this world," as I call my re-entry into society in late 2004, acceptance of my circumstances and of the people in my life has been a key to being able to cope on a daily basis, to allowing my life to be in flow, and to staying out of anger, bitterness, or regret.

To keep from becoming a prisoner of anyone or anything, I need to stay conscious of my circumstances and the people in my life. Once I accept the reality of "what is," I can choose whether or not to accept the situation or people "as is," to change something within the situation, the relationship, or myself, or to leave the situation or relationship.

The following exercises will help guide you through this process in your own life.

EXERCISE: Accept Your Circumstances

Not acknowledging or accepting the reality of your situation keeps you in a constant struggle against your life. It holds you hostage, creates resentment, and drains enormous amounts of energy. Resistance to reality is a major contributor to stress in your life. When you begin to acknowledge and accept "what is" in your life, then you can begin to open to the possibilities, options, and opportunities that are before you.

Make a list of circumstances in your life that are currently causing you to feel unhappy, angry, frustrated, or depressed.

Meditate for a few moments on each item on the above list, asking yourself the following questions. Jot notes down if you like, without editing yourself:

• What are the facts of the situation or my circumstances?

- Who or what am I blaming for this situation?

When you're in a situation you don't like or want, you have two options: leave it or accept it. After acceptance, either change can be made within that circumstance or situation, or you can choose to stop worrying, fretting, and wasting energy wishing it weren't so.

Acceptance is where most people run into greatest difficulty and they make their own lives miserable by resenting, resisting, and fighting their circumstances. You know you've accepted your circumstances when there is no more emotion around the situation. Then you are ready to make change.

===============

Review your list of circumstances. Go through each one and determine:

- Can you leave the situation? Put an "L" next to these items.

- If so, what would it take? If what it takes to leave the situation is not something you are willing or able to do, then this is not a viable option. Continuing to consider it only keeps you in another state of paralysis.

- Do you need to accept it as is? Put an "A" next to these items. Meditate on each one around the theme of accepting it. Note what thoughts, emotions, or ideas come up.

Let it go now and come back to this section in a few days. Reread the situations you need to accept. Has your resistance to accepting eased up?

When you no longer feel emotion or a "yes, but..." around the situation, make some notes here on what possibilities open up with the acceptance of the circumstances. What changes can you make now within the situation?

EXERCISE: Expectations

When your expectations of others do not match the reality of who they are, there is a disconnect. They will disappoint you, annoy you, or let you down. This will lead you to blame, and very likely, to arguments. Stop the cycle.

———

Look closely at the people in your life who annoy you or disappoint you. What is the reality of who they are?

When you accept this reality, what thoughts, ideas, or feelings come up for you? Are there changes you can make in the relationship?

NOTES

5TH PRINCIPLE:
CHOOSE YOUR RESPONSE

Between stimulus and response there is a space.
In that space is our power to choose our response.
In our response lies our growth and our freedom.
—Viktor Frankl

n Chikurubi, I was not able to change my circumstances, and thus had to accept certain unpleasant things in life (*The 4th Principle: Accept Your Circumstances*). But I also learned that I could choose how I responded to my circumstances, and in this way, I was free. By changing my response, I changed my entire experience, even of the most unpleasant things. I demonstrated this with the food.

Here's another example: Chikurubi was built in a hexagon. With my luck, my cell was in the middle, opposite the entrance. So when the guards entered the prison to beat us every day, it didn't matter if they went left or right, it took them about two hours to beat their way to my cell.

Every morning for two hours or so, I had to sit there in my cell, listening to people getting beaten, to the screams and cries and moans getting closer and closer to my cell. As the noise got nearer, everyone in our cell would become more and more agitated. Man, by the time they opened that door, I would be a wreck. My stomach would be churning, I'd be sweating, I'd have a headache. For years, my morning routine consisted of two hours of stressing, then a beating, then blind anger and rage. It occurred to me one day that it wasn't the beatings that were going to kill me; it was the *waiting* for the beatings that was going to kill me.

After I had the revelation about the food and me as the Determining Factor in how I experienced my circumstances, I realized that the beatings were just like the food. I couldn't change the situation. I couldn't leave it or hide or run. I had to acknowledge the facts of the situation: the authorities had complete and utter charge over me and could do with me as they wanted. I had to accept the situation: I was going to get beaten every day. So I had to figure out how to deal with it.

As I stated in *The 4th Principle: Accept Your Circumstances*, the only thing we have control over is ourselves and how we respond. We are the Determining Factor in every situation or circumstance.

So, at Chikurubi, like it or not, all I had to work with was *me*.

I decided to try the same method with the beatings as I had with the food: to reprogram my mind. Every time I heard them coming, I decided I was going to say to myself, "Chill out. You can't run. You can't hide. It's gonna happen, so don't stress."

Have you ever told yourself not to worry? Oh, boy. Then you worry. Oh, man, trying to convince myself not to stress out was rough. But eventually, like the situation with the hunger, those words became a mantra.

One morning, the guards came, opened the door, beat us, and it was only as they were leaving that I realized, *I didn't hear them coming this morning.*

I was perplexed. I wondered, *How did I not hear these people coming?*

As holds true of so many things, the result of my efforts was not what I had expected, so I didn't recognize it for what it was at first. The next morning, the same thing occurred. I didn't remember hearing them coming and suddenly they were at the door.

And then I realized that once again, I had managed to change my thinking. I understood, *I may not be able to control my circumstances, but I can choose how I respond to my circumstances.*

I added another element. When they left, rather than spending the rest of the day plotting my revenge, I decided I would let it go. I'd tell myself, "It's over." There was nothing else productive I could do. But that way, I didn't ruin the rest of my day with feelings of hatred and violence.

In the beginning, my change in attitude made no difference to anybody but me, but what an enormous difference it made to me! I didn't sit and sweat for two hours prior to the beating and I didn't fume the rest of the day afterwards. I began to have a better sense of well-being. I found other things to think about. But mostly I stopped spending half my day in dread and fear and anger.

The experience taught me that what happens to me in life is not as important as how I respond to what happens to me. What a sense of freedom I had with this realization! That meant I was truly free, even in prison. I could control none of what was going on around me or to me. I wanted none of it, but I *could* control me, I could *choose my response.* I believe this is what allowed me to come out of that place not just having survived it, but with the capability to be resilient and thrive beyond it.

Months went by and one day, the guards came in, beat everybody else, didn't touch me and walked out. I thought to myself, *Wow, Christmas. They missed. First time.*

The next day, the same thing happened. Twice in a row to miss the one guy who stood out like a spotlight? What was going on? Going forward, the guards did not beat me during those morning group sessions. I'm not a scientist; all I can say is that somehow the fact that I had stopped fearing them had gotten transmitted to them and they stopped beating me. Perhaps the fun went out of it. I don't know.

Not only did I learn that I could choose my response, I also learned first hand that the old adage, "It takes two to tango" is true. In every situation, both parties have to play their roles in order for it to play out the same. But if one of the players changes his or her role—his or her response—it changes the game. With the beatings, the traditional role of the prisoner was to respond either with violence or to curl up in a ball and cower. The prisoner who responded with violence was met with more violence. The prisoner who curled up in a ball was a victim and got no mercy either. The prisoner who responded with neither, however, threw the perpetrators off.

Try an experiment. The next time you get into it with your spouse or partner or child or parent or co-worker, respond differently. Respond *indifferently*. What happens?

What is reprogramming your mind really all about? Choosing to respond differently than you normally do. The challenge comes in with the fact that your responses have been ingrained in you for so long, they have become automatic. But just as you trained yourself in one response, it is possible to train yourself in another.

This is what I mean when I say that happiness is a choice and that you are the Determining Factor in your own happiness. You get to choose how to respond to what's happening to you. You get to choose to be sad or happy, angry or joyful, a victim or a victor. You choose this state by choosing your response, regardless of what happens.

I'm not suggesting you deny your feelings or pretend to be happy when you are not. I'm suggesting quite the opposite—that you get really real and really authentic. I'm suggesting that you acknowledge that you are unhappy, accept that something is not right, then choose your response. Do you choose to be angry? That's fine. That's your choice. Does being angry make you feel better? Does it bring you joy? Does it resolve the situation? If so, then it was the appropriate response for the situation. If not, perhaps you want to choose another response and see what happens.

Just like the other Principles of forgiveness and acceptance, choosing your response takes practice until it becomes a way of life. You must first acknowledge and accept your situation or circumstances, using *The 4th Principle: Accept Your Circumstances*. This creates consciousness. If you are unconscious of reality, you are not conscious enough to choose your response to it, either.

EXERCISE: Choose Your Response

Reon demonstrated multiple times throughout his Chikurubi experience that we are the Determining Factor for every situation in our lives, because we get to choose how we respond to whatever is happening to us.

Using Reon's life as an inspiration, you can believe that changing how you respond is truly possible. No one says it's easy, though. Choosing one's response takes practice and time. It helps to think ahead about common situations or people in your life to which you have automatic responses you don't like, that you're not proud of, or that cause suffering to yourself and others. Consider a different response to utilize to change your experience.

———————

Review the list you wrote in the previous chapter about what circumstances you decided you need to accept. Below, write down how you normally respond to these circumstances. Now look at the list and your responses, and come up with some ideas on how you could respond differently.

CIRCUMSTANCE	OLD RESPONSE	NEW RESPONSE

Pick one of the situations and practice your desired, new response for one week. When you catch yourself reacting with your old response, simply acknowledge that you are acting out of habit and choose the response you want. Catching yourself in the old response is part of the practice of choosing a new response, so don't be discouraged when you catch yourself; instead, congratulate yourself for your consciousness!

After one week, review how you did. What changed?

Do you need more time? Remember: life is not instant pudding. Change doesn't happen in a snap. Reon shares that it took him months and even years to reprogram his thinking. Keep practicing. Choose this one new response until it becomes automatic. Then choose another to tackle.

NOTES

6TH PRINCIPLE:
LEAD BY EXAMPLE

Be the change you want to see in the world.
—Mahatma Gandhi

That filthy cell toilet drove me nuts. It was so disgusting. Oddly enough, after a while I didn't smell it. But the sight of the mess just drove me insane. I couldn't deal with it. I sat and fretted about it for years.

One day, I was sitting there looking at the mess, getting freaked out about it, and thought to myself: *Wait a minute. If that bugs you so much, do something about it, or shut up and stop obsessing about it. Simple. Ignore it or do something about it.*

But what could I do? I had no money to pay somebody to clean it up. I couldn't tell—or even ask— the guards to do it. I couldn't order or force my fellow prisoners to do it. All that left was...me. Once again, the Determining Factor.

That month, when we got our bit of water to clean ourselves, I stood up, took my portion and with my bare hands, I cleaned that mess. Now, I've done some pretty nasty jobs in my life but that one takes the cake. While I was cleaning, the whole cell went quiet and I could feel 49 pairs of eyes burning into my back. I just knew the collective thought going through the room was, "That honky has just flipped. He's just lost it." What sane person would clean that hole with his bare hands?

Nobody said a word. As I walked back to my place, no one even looked at me. No one wanted to provoke me if I had really gone nuts. Nobody ever said thank you. No one mentioned it. When I sat down and I looked at that place and it was clean, I thought, *Wow! That looks good.*

I knew it wasn't going to last, but for that moment, it felt good to have done something about it. The next month, I cleaned the hole in the floor that served as our latrine again. And again. I don't know how many times I did it—three times, four times. I cannot remember. But I kept on doing it. I didn't do it for anybody else. I didn't do it to prove a point. I did it for myself. It bothered me and when I cleaned it, I felt better.

One month, when I got my water and walked to that toilet, one of the other guys got up and said, "Reon, it's my turn. I'll do it." With his bare hands and his bit of water, he cleaned it. The following month, somebody else did. It became an unspoken agreement in that cell that each person would take a turn using his bare hands and his meager bit of water to clean that toilet.

That experience taught me a few things. First, that there is no more powerful way to lead than by example. Not by ordering or demanding or commanding—by doing.

It also taught me that, if something bothers you, *do* something about it or shut up. Don't sit around and complain and point out how bad or wrong or stupid something is. Take action or stop talking about it. Why should anyone else take action if you won't? And why are you waiting for someone else to take action about something that's bothering *you*? That is yet another way you give away your power to choose: by not taking action regarding something that bothers you and instead, waiting for someone else to do it.

I also learned that earning the respect of others comes from what we *do*, not what we *say*. If we are consistent with what we do, we can change people's perceptions of us.

When I entered that prison, I was the most reviled inmate there. Simply because I was a white Afrikaner, I was assumed to be a racist jerk. I had decades of South African government policy and practices going against me, along with a general negative perception of SA Special Forces. There was nothing I could say to these people that would lead them to believe otherwise about me. All I could do was demonstrate the true nature of my character by what I did in a consistent manner.

When I left that prison, there wasn't a prisoner or a guard who didn't cry and cheer for me to be leaving there alive.

EXERCISE: Lead by Example

Fortunately, you likely won't ever have to clean a dirty toilet with your bare hands. But every day, you probably complain about things you want to see changed or that you want others to do. Over time, the complaining or waiting for others to take action become habits. To affect change in your life, you need to nip these habits in the bud. Use Reon's story as a reminder when you feel like complaining.

Try this. The next time you find yourself complaining about something or someone, make a choice: do something or stop complaining. Every time you feel the urge to complain, first ask yourself what, if anything, you are willing to do to change the situation. If you are not willing to do anything, don't allow yourself to complain. Practice this for three days straight. Notice any shifts that take place in your life as a result.

Leading by example take conscious effort. Name something that bothers you that you'd like to change, but are waiting for someone else to do it.

Are you willing to do it yourself?

If so, what action can you take?

Make a list of things you want others in your life (children, parents, spouse/ significant other, friend, co-worker) to do.

Are you willing to do these things first? Pick one, do it first, and see how others in your life respond.

NOTES

7TH PRINCIPLE:
PRACTICE
"THIS IS SUFFICIENT"

═══════════════════

Wake at dawn with a winged heart
and give thanks for another day of loving.
—**Kahlil Gibran**

There is a great illness in our society: want. As long as we want, we feel unhappy, unfulfilled, restless, empty.

I was without a lot of things in that prison. But strangely enough, over time, what I had was somehow enough. In fact, when I came back to "this world," as I call the outside, all the stuff was overwhelming. In that place, my perception changed of what it is "I need."

The fact is, we humans really need very little. I've proven that. The challenge is that we confuse *need* with *want.* The difference between needing and wanting is a simple concept most children study in elementary school as they learn about cultures around the world. But why do none of us remember it or practice it? The single greatest factor in unhappiness is want: wanting more than we have, what we don't have, or what we cannot have. Want is a bottomless pit.

I wanted more food. I wanted different food. I wanted better food. As long as I didn't have what I wanted, I felt the lack. I was hungry. Starving, in fact, is what I told myself. But as I looked at the facts, as stated in *The 4th Principle: Accept Your Circumstances*, I discovered that I was not starving, because I was still alive. I was simply wanting something else, and more of it.

As I worked with my "mantra" of "I'm not hungry," I believe what I was really communicating to myself was, "This is sufficient." "This is enough." As I reprogrammed my mind to accept that what I had was sufficient to sustain me, the ever-present gnawing hunger faded.

The human mind is an amazing thing. It must be trained, however, otherwise it will run us ragged with all its tangents and demands and perceptions. How do we train it? We start by staying aware of what our mind is telling us.

Yours is likely telling you each day that you are unhappy because something is *lacking* in your life, such as money, status, or a relationship. Where do these thoughts come from? They often come from your culture and your society. The entire consumer society is built on want, especially wanting things you don't really need. That's why you often feel empty shortly after you get something you thought you wanted.

I'm not telling you to deny yourself, to settle for less, or that getting rid of everything you have is the key to happiness. My advice is this: if you have things that you've earned, enjoy them. But if having them, maintaining them, or holding on to them causes you anxiety or keeps you awake at night, get rid of them. So many people tell me, "I own two houses." "I own this awesome sports car." "I own this company." No, those things own *you* if they cause you continued anxiety or sleepless nights. And if *wanting* also causes you sleepless nights or unhappiness, consider changing your thought patterns around want.

I wanted more food. As long as I believed I *needed* what I *wanted*, I was unfulfilled. When I changed that thinking to be that I *had* what I *needed*, a shift happened within me. Nothing else changed. *I* changed. I shifted my perception; I changed my attitude. I moved from, "I want" to, "This is sufficient." For me, it was a paradigm shift that has become permanent and impacts the way I look at the world and live my life.

Oh, I still want things. But I don't confuse *wanting* them with *needing* them to feel complete, happy or fulfilled. Thus, I can be happy if I have what I want...or don't have what I want. I am content.

EXERCISE: Practice "This is Sufficient"

Contentment is not the same as complacency. Complacency begets boredom, sluggishness, and mediocrity. Contentment brings feelings of happiness, peace, and fulfillment. As long as you are feeling lack somewhere in your life, you are restless and uneasy in your own skin.

Sometimes want can be a positive factor in your life. For instance, a longing in one's soul for something deeper and more meaningful in life keeps you seeking divine truth. That's not the same kind of want to which Reon is referring in this Principle. You need to separate the call of your soul from the call of your ego.

━━━━━━━━━

Journal on the areas in your life where you feel you are in want, or where you feel you have less than you want.

Look at each one and ask yourself, "Is this a longing from my soul or my ego?" "Is this a necessity that I need to survive, or is it merely a want?" If it's a longing from your soul and/or a life necessity, what can you do to address the lack?

Pick one that is not a necessity and create a mantra, like Reon's "This is sufficient; I'm not hungry," that you can say to yourself to begin to reprogram your mind around this issue of want or lack.

My mantra around _____ (area of lack) is (write it out here):

Practice every day. Every time you think the "want" thoughts, say your mantra. Do this for one week. Revisit this page one week from today. What has shifted for you?

Need more time? Give it another week or even a few. When you are ready, pick another area from your original list, develop a simple mantra, and practice consistently for a week.

As Reon pointed out in **The 2nd Principle: Love and Serve Others**, an effective way to stop obsessing about your own life and what you lack is by serving others. Review your list from The 2nd Principle exercise. What act of service can you pursue instead of indulging or wallowing in your want?

NOTES

8TH PRINCIPLE:
UNDERSTAND
THERE IS NO "THERE"

Peace is not the absence of conflict from life,
but the ability to cope with that conflict.
—Unknown

For twelve years and eight months, all my prayers, hopes, wishes, everything I asked for, lived for, prayed for was for that door to open. I thought, *If I can survive this prison, if that door can just open, if I can just get back to my homeland, nothing in life can ever be a problem again. If I can survive this cancer and this prison and walk out of here, how can life ever be a hassle again?*

I believed that if only I could get out of Chikurubi and back to South Africa and my people, all my problems would be over. I was stunned to arrive where I wanted to be and find that my challenges weren't over, but rather just beginning in a whole different way. While before I had been imprisoned, tortured, beaten, and kept in abominable conditions, once home, I was jobless, homeless, in a country that didn't want me, without family, friends or employable skills. Oh, and extremely ill.

This taught me that even after all I had learned through my experiences in Chikurubi, I still had more to learn. Perhaps the biggest lesson of all: there is no "there." There is no moment we reach when all hassles and problems fade away and life is perfect. The only time I'm certain that happens is when we're dead.

In the meantime, life brings challenges and hassles and problems. It's a given. If we can accept this, we can learn to stop being surprised or upset or shocked or hurt when life happens. We can learn to roll better with the punches.

We always think that if I can only get "there"—"there" being an infinite number of wishes: surviving until the door opens, getting an extra 10,000 bucks, becoming the manager, snagging a younger wife or a richer husband, getting a faster car or a bigger house. "If I can only get 'there,'" we tell ourselves, "then life will be good. Then I'll be happy," or "then I won't be stressed."

Another version of this is, "I'll be happy when..." Insert anything you are waiting for in the future: "the kids move out," "I pay off the mortgage," "I get out of debt," "I get this promotion," "This project is over," "I meet my soul mate," and so on.

I'm here to tell you first hand: there is no "there." Only here, now.

There are several lessons within this. The first is that with a "I'll be happy when..." mindset, you put off being present by constantly waiting for the future. More importantly, you put off feeling happy in the present because you are constantly waiting for something better in the future.

Furthermore, you push away happiness and contentment now, because you think it's coming in greater abundance later, in the form of something, someone, or somewhere different than what you have or where you are now. But what if tomorrow never comes...

UNDERSTAND THERE IS NO "THERE" | 103

and you missed today? Because, in fact, that's what does happen. Tomorrow never comes, because when it does, it's today! Yet you miss today, looking for tomorrow. Sounds pretty crazy when put that way, doesn't it?

But we are all doing this, which is why there's an epidemic of unhappiness in our society. There are so many people living in this world who are so consumed with regretting the past and worrying about the future that they're never present. They don't enjoy anything.

The past is in the past and it should stay there. We can learn from it, but we can't change it. And why worry about the future? It might never happen. We're missing all the beauty around us now.

We delude ourselves into thinking that something, someone, or somewhere else will make us happier, more successful, more fulfilled, more peaceful than we currently are...and when we get there, we are disappointed to find it's not the case. This keeps us eternally searching, unhappy, unfulfilled, and disappointed. We also may start to think that life is "out to get us" or that we "get all the bad breaks." No, my friend. We just get life.

Every morning, I awake before sunrise and go outside to greet the day. In those wee hours, I spend time being grateful that I am free, that I am alive, and that I am able to go outside. I also spend time psyching myself up to go through another day, because I still have my hassles, my health issues, and my financial issues.

The challenge that stands before each of us is to choose to go through the day, *despite* knowing there will be hassles. We get to exercise our Power of Choice in how we will respond to those hassles, however, and in that way, get to choose how we will experience the day. Remember:

Peace is not the absence of conflict from life,
but the ability to cope with that conflict.

EXERCISE: Understand There Is No "There"

Perhaps the rudest awakening for Reon came after prison, when his greatest hope and wish came true—the door of his prison cell opened and he became a free man again. Like all of us, Reon believed that if he could only get "there," nothing in life could be a hassle again. But the truth, he found, is that there is no "there" in life—a place, time, status, or person—where everything is perfect.

Whenever you reach the goal you are striving for, whenever a wish comes true, it's not the end and happily ever after, but a whole new set of challenges to overcome. That's life. When you realize this, you can stop waiting for life to begin or to get better later, and you can also stop the cycle of disappointment at it not being all you thought it would be when you got "there."

It's the human instinct of continually striving to get "there" at some point in the future that keeps you unhappy here, now, and usually disappointed "there," then.

━━━━━━

Make a list of what you tell yourself will make you happy in the future if you have more of, less of, or different than what you have right now.

Now make a list of what you DO have, right now, that you are grateful for.

List your most common, "When I get 'there', then..." or "I'll be happy when..." thoughts.

By living in "When I get 'there'" or "I'll be happy when" thoughts, what are you missing in your life right now?

What do these exercises reveal for you that you would like to change?

NOTES

9TH PRINCIPLE:
STOP WHYNING!

*Courage is nothing less than the power to overcome
danger, misfortune, fear, injustice, while continuing to
affirm inwardly that life with all its sorrows is good;
that everything is meaningful
even if in a sense beyond our understanding...*
—Dorothy Thompson

During my first years in Chikirubi, I repeatedly asked, *Why?
Why me?* As years of torture, beatings, starvation rations,
mortal illness, and inhumane conditions wore on, I began to
wonder, *Why do I keep surviving?* When I was released and everything
looked dismal, I thought again, *Why? Why did I survive all this?*

But then I decided that "Why?" was not the right question. The
better question was, "What for?" *For what purpose am I suffering? For
what purpose have I survived?"*

What for? To share what I learned with you.

Since I was released in 2004, I've been traveling the world speaking to audiences of people like yourself. I've spoken to government leaders, defense forces, students, sports teams, cancer survivors, corporate leaders, gang members, company employees, moms, dads, kids, prisoners, and war veterans. If you had told me seven years ago that I'd be traveling the world speaking to hundreds of thousands of people, telling my story, I would not have believed you.

As discussed in *The 5th Principle: Choose Your Response*, what happens in your life is not as important as what you *do* with what happens in your life. You can sit down and be a victim or you can stand up and be a victor. You can choose to learn from your mistakes or simply choose to continue to make mistakes for no purpose.

Some months ago, I met a Tibetan Buddhist monk at a monastery in rural Thailand. He said to me, "Some people choose to go into suffering to reach enlightenment. Others are chosen to be put into suffering to reach enlightenment."

And still others, I would add based on my observations, just suffer for no apparent gain.

The majority of people fall into this last category.

Everyone suffers on some level; it's the human condition. But at the first signs of suffering—which is to say, to feeling uncomfortable physically, mentally, emotionally, or spiritually—most people's response is to run, to do whatever it takes to get out of the situation, and stop the discomfort. That's human nature. But usually running from the discomfort doesn't get the desired results. It just keeps you on the run, dissatisfied, continually searching, continually trying to get "there" to reach eternal happiness.

I believe there is a grand misperception in our world: the belief that the road to happiness should be a comfortable one and that *dis*comfort signifies something is wrong, that you are somehow failing at life. This belief includes thinking that when you are not getting everything you want, that when things go wrong, you aren't doing life "right." My experience is that things "going wrong"—i.e., suffering—is the flame that transmutes our existence into gold. Without suffering, there is no transformational fire.

You get to choose whether the suffering you experience has purpose or if it's senseless. You determine that by choosing how you *respond* to suffering.

What one does with the suffering that occurs in his or her life is the dividing line between those who are at peace, those who do not merely survive, but thrive, between those who are resilient...and those who live in a hell of restlessness, anger, revenge, and ultimate self-destruction in some form.

An almost automatic response to suffering is asking "Why?" That question, however, has a tone of both blame and self-pity. It is limiting. It also implies, "I'm too good for this. Let it happen to anyone but me."

The better question to ask in the face of suffering is: *What for? For what purpose is this happening?* This simple shift in words creates a dramatic shift from a limiting mindset to one of possibility. As I changed the question to myself, I moved from self-pity to understanding that my *"what for"* was to share what I had learned with others, to help them live happier, more fulfilled, successful lives. This gave meaning to my suffering, which before had been senseless. I discovered there is always a *"what for"* surrounding the things that happen in my life...and there is for the things happening in your life, too. You simply need to ask the question: *What for?*

The answer may not readily present itself. It may not be understood for years. This goes back to the concept I shared in *The 3rd Principle: Perseverance*, about living in an instant-pudding world, expecting immediate results or answers. Sometimes, in an attempt to make sense of a current (seemingly) senseless situation, you start assigning meaning to it, or looking for "signs." Then everything becomes a "sign" and you are off and running on a tangent that you are driving, maybe even from your ego, instead of listening to what the Divine Source (whether you call that God, the Universe, your Inner Knowing, or some other name) has in store for you. What I am suggesting is that you ask, "What for?" when you experience suffering, then let the question go and stay open to how the answer takes form in your life.

That answer is not usually arrived at through intellectual explanation, especially if you are in the midst of suffering. More often, the answer reveals itself in an unexpected way, at an unexpected moment. You will know when it reveals itself, however.

I wasn't lying in my cell, asking myself what I was going to do with my suffering, plotting how I would create a "what for" to all of it by telling my story around the world. I had never heard of people who made a life or a living from speaking or who sold their "life rights" within hours of a crisis. I was mostly in perplexed despair when I tried to answer the "what for?" intellectually.

A few weeks after my release, however, I started receiving phone calls from churches, professional organizations, companies, and cancer survivor groups, among others, requesting that I share my story. My initial response was, "Everyone has a story. So what?" But the callers persisted until I finally said yes.

I've been speaking non-stop around the world since. I'm actually a reluctant speaker and have tried several times to find a different line of work. But every time I've tried to change careers, something has pushed me back into sharing my story. After a few years, even a stubborn Afrikaner like me gets the message.

EXERCISE: Stop WHYning!

What will you do with your suffering? How will you use it to shape you, to move you along the path that we call life? Reon clearly shows, again and again, that while you may not have chosen suffering, you can choose how you respond to it or what to do with your suffering. You can choose to find meaning in it, and you can thus come to a new level of comfort, joy, and peace. Or not. It's truly your choice.

=======

List three examples of "bad" or senseless things that have happened to you in the past that made you wonder at the time, "Why me? Why is this happening to me?"

Now look at each situation and ask yourself, "What for?" What purpose can you see in the situation? For instance, did it soften something in you that had heretofore been hard? Did it move you in a new direction in your career or personal life? What gifts can you identify were received from suffering?

Are you running from suffering right now? If you turn to face it, what would that feel like? Could you possibly stop running? What would it take?

What suffering in your life right now is causing you to ask, "Why me?"

Try asking, 'What for?" What ideas or thoughts come to you? Don't force meaning, just open to the possibility of there being meaning.

For the next month, every time you want to WHYne, instead ask, "What for?" and note what possibilities open up!

NOTES

10TH PRINCIPLE:
EXERCISE YOUR POWER OF CHOICE

In the long run, we shape our lives, and we shape ourselves. The process never ends until we die. And the choices we make are ultimately our own responsibility.
—Eleanor Roosevelt

The way you most often imprison yourself is by believing you have no choice. How often do you say, "I had no choice"? What I've learned is that there is *always* a choice; the disconnect is, you may not like the options, so you say there is no choice.

Other times, you give away your power to choose. "I can't decide. You choose," you say. Then you turn around and state, "I had no choice." Or you gripe about the choice someone else has made for you. You do this because you do not want to take responsibility for your life.

Other times you just aren't even aware that you're making choices. "I'm going to school because my parents make me." "I'm going to work because I have to." No. When you go to school or to work, when you physically show up there, you are actually *choosing* to go to school or work because you are there.

Don't imprison yourself with the myth that you are not choosing your life. Every moment of every day, you are faced with choices, and you are making them, often unconsciously. At any moment, your choice can change the course of your day, and over time, the course of your life. But too often, you give up the power to choose, or you choose unconsciously, and in this way, you give up your freedom and imprison yourself.

Another way you imprison yourself is by living in fear—fear of losing a job, fear of change, fear of losing a relationship, fear of failure, fear of losing your possessions. The list of fears goes on an on. Fear is a killer to success and joy. Fear paralyzes. Fear is contagious and poisonous.

Anger, revenge, lack of forgiveness, and blame are other jailers you may cling to as if they were lifesavers. In fact, they are life-destroyers. I know. I lived on hate, bitterness, and thoughts of revenge for the first several years of my time in Chikurubi. It took me years to figure out that those thoughts, not the people or the place I was, were going to destroy me.

We are all looking for a life of peace and happiness. It is a universal quest. I have found peace and happiness are not what many believe they are. They are not found in material things or even in another person. They are not a point we get to where there are no hassles or problems. A state of total peace and happiness is possible and can be achieved. This I know first hand. But it takes work and sacrifice. That state of peace and happiness cannot be bought, traded, or given. One has to earn it by working on and within oneself. It is not easily brought about. It takes time and effort. But we are all, each and every one of us, capable of reaching it. Peace and happiness are a state of mind and they are a choice.

How do you create a mindset that offers fertile ground for peace and happiness to grow?

To begin with, you have to understand what peace and happiness really are, and then where they come from: within. You have to understand and believe that you have it within you to be happy and at peace no matter what your circumstances are or where you might be. You have the choice to be happy or sad, at peace or upset, regardless of the world around you. Do you believe this?

In addition, you have to believe that there are no problems in life that cannot be solved or resolved. Otherwise, you will give up your goals and dreams too easily. Don't see problems; see solutions.

We often don't see solutions because they are not the solutions we want. It's like when we pray to God and think God is not answering our prayers. God always answer prayers, but most of the time, He does not provide the answer we want or expect, so we tell ourselves God is not answering.

That leads me again to expectations and disappointment. In my opinion, life, people, things, places, or God can't disappoint us. It is we who create disappointment through our expectations. We create expectations and then blame our disappointment on outside factors. "I expected the hotel to be nicer." "I expected him to be taller." "I'm disillusioned that she's not who I thought she was." "I'm disappointed my child didn't do better." "Parents are supposed to be perfect."

You may not be able to do away with expectations. But recognize that they are *your* expectations and see if that changes your relationship to disappointment and perhaps also eliminates some of the tendency to place blame.

Blame comes when you don't want to take responsibility for your actions, your life, or your choices. Do not imprison yourself by giving up your power to choose, including choosing to take responsibility for your life.

Of course, choices come with consequences. What I like about the Power of Choice is that if you make a poor choice, with consequences you do not like, you can choose again.

The most powerful tool in our human tool kit is the power to choose, *The Power of Choice*. I am here to tell you that it doesn't matter what your circumstances are, it doesn't matter what has happened in the past or what's happening to you right now. If you can just hold on to the knowledge that, "I can decide what I'm going do with this. I'm going to choose what I let this make me feel like," you are free.

Based on my experience of life, I believe you can really, truly choose happiness, despite your circumstances. Happiness doesn't always mean giddy, skipping, wild joy. Happiness is knowing you are free, that you are conscious, that you are choosing your responses, that you are choosing your life, and that when you make a choice that's not serving you, you can choose again.

The Power of Choice. You have it. Exercise it.

EXERCISE: The Power of Choice

Like Reon living in prison, you may think you have no choice about some aspect or even all of your life. But as Reon discovered that he could be free even while in prison, you, too, can be free, even when you do not like or want your situation. You do this by putting The 10 Principles into practice in your everyday life.

═══════════

Where in your life do you perceive that you "have no choice"?

Look more closely to find the choices within "no choice."

Identify where in your life are you giving away your Power of Choice.

Think about your day. What unconscious choices did you make today?

The goal of this book is not for you to get life "right," to never make a mistake again or to become enlightened. It's to help you to become conscious, which is to say, to become aware. You will have made great progress when you can simply catch yourself in the act of WHYning, in the act of blame, in the act of viewing yourself as trapped with no choices, and can acknowledge that that is what you are doing. Such recognition allows the opening for making different choices than the ones you are used to. Use Reon's story as a beacon to shine the light of consciousness into your own life.

Today, practice consciousness with regard to making choices. Every time you do something—brushing your teeth, taking a shower, going to work or school, making dinner—become conscious that you are doing it and that you are choosing to do it. Note below how your experience of your life might be different when you recognize that you're choosing every moment of your life.

NOTES

REON'S
CLOSING THOUGHTS

Through what I initially viewed as one of the worst fates possible, my life took a different turn from the track I was on several decades ago—a turn inward. The nearly thirteen years I spent in Chikurubi gave me the time to analyze my life, my fears, my thoughts, my choices, the state of who I'd become. I began to question the thought patterns I'd been taught, the rhetoric of the government I had served, and the purpose of war and violence. I contemplated the quest of humans for peace and happiness and the reasons we misunderstand and hate one another. And I thought a lot about God, in between arguing with Him and cursing Him.

I grew up with a God who sat in Heaven, waiting to pound me down with his fists every time I did something wrong. *Why is He so angry all the time?* I had wondered as a kid. *Why did He create us if He dislikes us so much?*

In the military, I started to question that God of my ancestors. We always had a chaplain who prayed over us before we headed into battle. The chaplain would ask God to protect us against our enemies and bring us back home safely and victorious. Yet, right across the border, another chaplain was praying over *his* soldiers, asking God to bring them—our enemies—back home safely and victorious. Was God supposed to choose sides? If so, how did He pick? We were certain we were in the right, and our enemies were just as certain they were in the right. Quite a quandary.

We are conditioned to be who we are and to believe and behave in the manner of our society and culture. Our society, culture, schools, religions, business cultures, and even families tend to teach us that there is only one truth, and that it is absolute. Is it really?

I had more than a decade with little to do other than thinking long and hard about what is "true." I discovered that there are many versions of the truth. I say truth is in the eye of the beholder, for I learned that two people can look at the exact same thing or situation and see two completely different circumstances or events. It is often because of our inability to tolerate the differences in each other's truths or to see life from another's perspective that we have so much unhappiness in our lives.

The God I met in Chikurubi was not the guy with the fists or the one who picks sides. I met a tolerant, compassionate, loving, forgiving God in Chikurubi, and came to know Him up close and personal during my 4,620 "Dark Nights of the Soul." I saw Him in an unexpected kindness risked by a guard and in a compassionate word from a fellow prisoner. I heard Him in the letters from my support group and felt Him opening my heart as I chose to serve those less fortunate around me.

I consider myself to be "spiritual" rather than "religious." Too many horrible things have been done throughout the ages in the name of God and religions. Too many wars have been fought in His name and for various "Chosen People." In my opinion, we are all "Chosen People." Not one of us is better than another.

Ultimately, *you* choose your experience of life by choosing your state of mind. Nobody and nothing in this world can make you happy. Things, people, places, and circumstances can add to your happiness, but they cannot make you happy. Only you can make you happy.

Likewise, no one can live your life for you. No one can make your choices for you. No one can take responsibility for your life. Every moment of every day is filled with choices. It is up to you—and only you—to make your choices in each moment, to choose again and again how you will respond to your circumstances. There is no point where you are "home free." You need to continue to practice your Power of Choice every day for the rest of your life. It's challenging and difficult, but the reward is complete and total freedom, no matter your circumstances.

If I, an uneducated soldier, can come to understand this and accomplish what I have over these past years since "coming back into the world," imagine how much more you can understand and accomplish in your life and in this world.

Remember this. Remember my story. Set yourself free.

ABOUT THE AUTHORS

Reon Schutte is an internationally renowned inspirational speaker who has shared the story of his triumphant personal life journey in person with more than 1 million people around the globe. Originally from South Africa, Reon now is a citizen of the world, living and taking his message where he is called. This is his first book.

Maggie Kuhn Jacobus is an award-winning author, journalist, and freelance writer, with expertise in the areas of spirituality and wellness. This is her fourth book. She holds both a bachelor's degree and a master's degree from Northwestern University's Medill School of Journalism, and is also a certified life coach. She currently resides in Milwaukee, WI with her three teenage boys, Ryan, Michael and Will.

For information about personal or executive coaching with Reon, as well as workshops and upcoming webinars on The Ten Principles, please visit www.reonschutte.com.

ABOUT THE POWER OF CHOICE FOUNDATION

The Power of Choice Foundation is an all-volunteer 501(c)3 non-profit organization. Its purpose is to provide grants and programming to charitable organizations around the world that encourage and foster self-reliance, personal responsibility, and the concept of The Power of Choice with their constituents.

Please visit www.ThePowerOfChoice.org for more information.

Printed in the USA
CPSIA information can be obtained
at www.ICGtesting.com
JSHW082353140824
68134JS00020B/2064